TIN CAN
SAILOR

C. SCHIPPOREIT

FOREWARD

This story, Tin Can Sailor, was written for a number of reasons. Personal memory of my brother Bill is limited to what I recall during the two times that I saw him, which was very early in my lifetime. On both occasions, he showed me what a caring person he was. Later when I shared plans to write about him, my sister Jeanie asked me to do all I could to illustrate how generous and loving he was to everyone during the time he lived. I have tried to do this.

The reason why most all of the names in my story are changed is because of my relationship with my family, as fractured as that might have been, before they returned to my life. I gave myself permission to portray them as I wanted them to be, and name changes made this somehow easier. I do hope that all who read my story, and in particular my family, will try to understand and accept my choices. In actuality, the family name was Persson before it was changed to Strand many, many years ago in Sweden!

This story is "historical fiction." It is based and documented factually. Other segments are written from wherever my imagination took me. I tried to portray my birth family as "normal" as I hoped they might be, yet understanding that they were not perfect. As my writing progressed, I began to feel more comfortable with the characters that I wrote about and long held undercurrents of pain and misunderstandings were eased.

My dear husband, Marty, who once served as a "shore-duty sailor" patiently answered so many questions that I had about basic training, uniforms, Navy vocabulary and so forth. So many, many times when I faltered, he was there to offer encouragement. Without his help, I could never have written Tin Can Sailor.

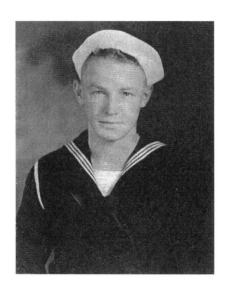

Dedicated to the memory of my brother,
Nels Axel William Strand, and all the valiant
men who served aboard the
USS Preston-DD379
Corrine (Chris) Schipporeit

CHAPTER 1:

NELS AXEL WILLIAM

The pains had gone on for what seemed like days, and yet Karin's body could not or would not release this tiny new life that struggled so to break free from within her. Lars' mother had been with the family since the first part of March to prepare the meals and to care for the children; Anna, who wasn't yet three and the firstborn son Karl, who was almost grownup at the age of five. From the time that Karl was old enough to know where the woodpile was, it became his job to see that kindling was always brought into the house. Every morning and evening Karin took Karl with her to help as she did the chicken chores. These simple responsibilities most often given to older children of that era, had shortened Karl's carefree childhood days at play. He looked forward to the times when his grandmother came to stay with the family. Far-Mor Gertrude helped him through his chores and she always made sure to prepare tårta, his very favorite dessert, each time that she came to visit.

Lars stepped away from the bedside for a moment. He had been alternately wiping Karin's brow and squeezing her hands tightly as each of her anguished spasms began, reached its peak, and wound down again. Karin relaxed and rested as she could to ease the process. Through the kitchen window, the early morning sun was just beginning to send color into the day.

Far-Mor Gertrude stood by the small black cooking stove. She reached for the enameled coffeepot, and poured a cup of steaming encouragement for her son. She handed the chipped blue cup to Lars and asked softly, "Do you think I should go for the doctor?"

Slowly and silently Lars nodded assent, and Gertrude hastily threw her shawl over her shoulders and stepped out of the door. A short while later, she and Dr. Axel Jonsson returned, in time to observe Karin and Lars working through yet another tormented pang.

Anna had heard the door open when her grandmother and the doctor returned and was sitting up in her trundle bed rubbing her eyes. Gertrude crossed the room to the little girl, gently laid her back down in bed and pulled the quilt up to cover the child's body; all the while hoping to encourage more sleep and to muffle Anna's ears against the sounds of childbirth. The little boy sleeping in the bed above and to the side of Anna was oblivious to any of the commotion going on in the room. Lars often remarked that the house could blow away over Karl's head and he would not hear it.

Dr. Jonsson plopped his black valise on the chair by Karin's bedside and began to extract the tools and medication he needed to facilitate the passage of life into the world. Karin glanced at the doctor in grateful recognition as her jaw remained painfully clenched, holding back any words she might wish to say.

"Well, now, little mother," Dr. Jonsson began. "What seems to be the problem? You should have had this "borning" all finished by the time I got here. You've already done this before by yourself." He added to tease a bit, "Surely you know how it's done by now, or did you just want to see my handsome face today?"

Karin closed her eyes to shut out Dr. Jonsson's words as once again a pain began to wrench her forward. Yet once more she struggled to the peak of pain and slowly slid back down again.

"Oh, the wonder of it all," Dr. Jonsson began. "It's quite like the ocean waves growing wide and tall, then dropping back again. The baby is very close now, dear", he continued. "Just once or twice more."

Lars was more than ready for this baby to make its appearance. The other births had gone much easier. In fact Karin's previous labors were all over in a few hours. He wondered to himself why this time it was so difficult. Was there something wrong with the baby? Even little Justa, the premature baby boy who had remained with them for only a few short weeks, came into the world much easier than this child was doing.

"Please God," he began to pray silently, and scarcely having started his prayer, another sound came from the bed as the first cries of a new infant broke into the room.

"Hello, hello, little man," Dr. Jonsson cried. "We're awfully glad you're here, but did you have to make such a commotion in coming?"

"Oh, Lars, we have another son," Karin weakly murmured. Tenderly Lars brought her hand to his lips. "Yes, we do," Lars answered. As Lars gazed at his new little son, now resting on Karin's belly, he added, "And he appears to be full grown already."

"Poppa, poppa," came the call from Anna. "Can I wake up now? Can I see the baby?" she asked. Quickly Far-Mor went to the little girl and took her into her arms. Lifting Anna gently, she took the child to her mother's bedside to see the baby.

"He looks all funny," Anna said. "Well, he needs a bath," Far-Mor answered. "Then we must get his gown and a diaper," she went on.

"He'll look much better when he's cleaned up and dressed," Lars added. "Here, Anna, why don't you sit on my lap while Far-Mor takes care of him?"

Grandmother Gertrude took the infant child from Karin and quickly bathed all sign of prenatal existence from his newborn body. She dressed him in the little white gown that Karin had prepared for the baby, all the while humming a comforting lullaby that only his ears might hear.

"Lars," Far-Mor Gertrude began, "you are right. This baby is nearly full-grown already. He won't be long in this gown. Karin must get to her needle and thread very soon."

Dr. Jonsson completed the final care of Karin and began repacking his bag, getting ready to leave. Karin was quietly resting now, a contented smile on her face.

"Well, have you a name for this little boy?" Dr. Jonsson asked. Karin opened her eyes to look at the doctor as she replied. "We had thought that if our new child was a son we would name him Nels. And I do so like the name William. But we need another name too."

"I'd be quite proud if "Axel" would be a part of his name, Mrs. Persson," Dr. Jonsson volunteered.

And so it was that Nels Axel William was the name agreed upon. This fine, strong name, and his birth date of March 23, 1919, appeared on all the legal and church records but only his parents remembered how the name came to be. Everyone just called him Bill.

CHAPTER 2:

GOING TO AMERICA

Conversation about going to America had been in the air even before the birth of Nels Axel William. Lar's brother Otto had emigrated in 1913 and another brother, Sander, two years later. Their sister Gerda had gone to America also and was living on a farm in Minnesota with her husband Carl and their family.

The new baby took much of Karin's time even though he was a very contented infant. All could see that he was strong and healthy, growing visibly day-by-day. Karin cherished the moments spent holding and nursing her little son as she watched Anna happily playing with her doll.

"My baby is named Bill," Karin said to Anna one day. "What is your baby's name?" The little girl quickly answered, "My baby is a girl and her name is Inga." Karin smiled at her young daughter, amused by Anna's imagination.

The months passed quickly and one evening in October, Lars came home from work lugging a cart on which a large wooden trunk was loaded. Karl held the door open and Lars eased the trunk into the house.

"Here you are, Karin," he called. "This will surely be big enough to carry our treasures and possessions to America." Karin turned away from setting the table for supper, in time to witness the commotion and visibly assess the wooden container.

"Well, I guess we're really going," she replied. She had hoped so much that this move was not going to happen, but seeing the wooden trunk made her realize that it was very real, and she was not going to be able to change things.

Lars walked outdoors to place the cart closer to the house for the night. He wished above everything that Karin would share his enthusiasm about going to America. She had not said a word last month when he came home with their ticket for passage on the White Star Lines. Lars had hardly been able to contain his excitement when he picked up the ticket. He had read the information over and over again, marveling at how it had come to be.

An agent of the First National Bank of had prepared the arrangements for passage to St. Peter, Minnesota. The ocean fare from Malmo, Sweden was $275, and the railroad fare from New York was $108.37. Lars would be working for Mr. Larson in Minnesota for a very long time to pay off the passage expense note, but since he was only twenty-seven, he didn't view this as a problem. He'd work forever if that was what it took to live out his dream. It wasn't long before the packing process began and Karin could see that they would need one more trunk to hold items they planned to take with them to America. A friend had given Lars an old suitcase for the clothing they would need to use in their travels. Far-Mor Gertrude donated a valise that she had stored away in the barn rafters.

November 6, 1919 arrived before they realized it and early in the morning the young family with two trunks, two suitcases, a smaller valise, and three children in tow made their way to the train station. Far-Mor Gertrude also went with them on the train ride to Malmo. They all stayed overnight in a hotel there and the next day Lars and his family boarded a ferryboat for the ride to Kopenhamn in Denmark. Far-Mor Gertrude stood on the dock watching and waving until the ferryboat took them from her sight. In Kopenhamn they boarded another train, and in a short time this train itself was placed on another ferryboat to be carried to the next island. The journey continued from island to island several times until the train and passengers arrived at their destination, Esbjerg, Denmark.

The family did not sleep at all during the train and ferry rides across Denmark. The excitement of this new experience was much too exhilarating to waste on sleep. The next morning they embarked on a passenger boat and by 11:00 AM, had set sail for England. The following morning they arrived in Harwich. Once there, they had to walk two miles to the train station where they got on a train taking them to London and then on to Southampton.

By this time, the adventure and excitement had begun to wear on everyone. Everyone, that is, except baby Bill. He remained as content and happy as he had always been at home in his cradle. Karin mused to herself that this child had been born to see the world.

While in Malmo, Lars introduced himself to a man who was also traveling to America. Mr. Lindgren had quickly become a friend and proved invaluable in assisting the Persson family on their journey. He helped them find a hotel in Southampton where they would remain for three days before boarding the larger ship that would take them across the ocean to America. Arrangements were made to send their trunks ahead to the dock where they would be placed on board, prior to the time the family embarked. Karin was uncomfortable having to let the trunks out of sight in this way. She was certain that their "treasures" and possessions would be lost forever, yet she was grateful for the opportunity to rest for a while in this hotel. She so worried that one of the children would become separated from them as they went from train to ferry to train to ship, and her worries were not completely groundless as it was here in Southhampton that Karl struck off on his own adventure.

The morning they were to board their ship, Karl disappeared. Karin and Lars had busied themselves repacking the suitcases, making sure that all their belongings were included within the various cases. When the travel preparations were finished, Lars opened the door of their room and Karl stepped out ahead of the family. As they walked down the hall towards the front door of the hotel, nobody noticed when Karl ran ahead of the family, out the door, and in a flash, was gone.

Mr. Lindgren joined them in the hall and greeted them, "How is everyone this morning?" Turning to Anna he said, "Are you all ready for a big boat trip?" Then looking about he continued, "Where is young Mr. Karl?"

Karin's heart fell as she realized her young son was nowhere to be found, and time was short. They should have been at the dock by now, getting ready to board the large ship that would take them to America. Immediately Lars turned to Karin and said, "You wait here by the hotel door. Mr. Lindgren and I will look for Karl."

Anna began to cry for her brother and Karin was not far from tears herself. The baby was gurgling and cooing to his mother, as if to soothe her worry. The two men returned in just a few minutes with Karl in tow. He had followed his nose to a bakery just two doors down from the hotel. A bakery worker had softened to the little "Swedish beggar" and Karl was happily chewing on a piece of freshly baked bread as he was being returned to the group.

"Oh, Karl," Karin began. "Why did you leave us? I was afraid that you were forever lost," she gently scolded.

"But, Mama," Karl answered tearfully. "I was hungry and the bread smelled so good."

"Never mind now," Lars spoke to both. "The lost is found and we must hurry or the ship will leave without us." Quickly the group hurried along the way to the dock, seeing many more immigrant families laden with bags and valises, their children in tow, heading in the same direction.

At the sight of the huge ship with shining black smokestacks high on her decks, Karin was once again struck with apprehension.

All throughout Lars' planning their journey, she comforted herself by thinking that she would wake up to find it was all a dream, but now gazing up at the large ship, she understood that this was reality. They were really going to sail across the wide, wide ocean and she would never again see her beloved Sweden. She could hardly bear her sadness.

Mr. Lindgren said the ship was called the "Adriatic". Karin could see the name printed on the side of the ship. She knew this vessel would remain forever imprinted in her memory.

In a short time they worked their way up the gangplank and found a place back from the railing on the deck. Lars was hopeful that he might be able to see around the passengers at the rail and watch the sights of England fade from view.

When all the passengers and cargo were safely on board, the ship slowly pulled away from the dock. Lars nearly burst with exhilaration when they were finally underway, but Karin's attention was only on her children. She would not let Karl out of her sight even though Lars had joked that the little boy surely wouldn't be running away once they were on board the ship.

After the last bit of land had disappeared, the family made their way below deck to the small cabins designated for third class passengers. As they neared the door to their particular cabin, Karl cried out, "This door looks just like the one on Far-Mor's "garderob." Soon they had their smaller suitcases stowed under the bunks, and all settled down into the rhythm of the ocean. They ventured out later to the community dining room for their evening meal, then returned to the confines of "grandmother's closet" before preparing to go to bed for the night.

The ship sailed all that day and by evening of the next day, they were anchored at sea near Cherbourg, France. The Adriatic was to put on additional passengers here, but rough seas had prevented the small tender originally sent out, to complete the mission. These people had to be returned to shore and placed on a larger boat which made its way through the churning waters to the Adriatic's side. Once these new passengers were safely on board, the Adriatic headed for the open sea and the journey to America.

Karin did not adjust well to life on the sea. Her only bit of relief from continual seasickness came when she was able to make her way to the deck and catch a breath of fresh air. Anna unfortunately shared her mother's discomfort. Several times a day Lars took Karl up on deck and they passed their time tossing small matchboxes or orange peelings into the ocean and watching them quickly disappear. By the time they had been sailing for three days, Anna developed her sea legs and was happily joining them in this activity.

They had been at sea for over a week when one afternoon Anna asked her mother to help her in going down the passageway to the toilet. Karin had slept most of that day and was feeling somewhat better than she had when this voyage began. Together they made their way to the lavatory. Anna had taken her doll with her and entered the stall carrying Inga. In a short time she opened the door and tearfully cried out to her mother, "Inga fell into the potty." Quickly Karin stepped in, retrieved the doll and went at once to the sink to begin washing her off. All the while Anna was sobbing over the incident.

"Don't cry, Anna," Karin comforted. "Inga has had a nice bath in the sink and as soon as she gets dried, she will be just like new." Together they returned to their quarters and by the next day, Inga was dry and just like new, as Karin had promised.

Two days later, in mid afternoon, the passengers huddled by the railing for their first glimpse of the New York skyline. They did not leave the ship at Ellis Island to be processed. Instead they were vaccinated on board and all the necessary papers were filled out and completed. Once this was finished, the ship was allowed to dock and the travelers began to disembark. They were then directed to waiting ferry boats that would take them a short distance across New York harbor to New Jersey.

After being at sea for nine days, nobody was anxious to get aboard another boat even though they could see their destination in the distance. But onward the passengers plodded and the short ferry ride was over quickly. Once back on land, they made their way towards the train terminal. Karin was holding Bill and with her free hand she had a tight grip on Karl. She was not going to risk having him get away from the family as he had done in Southhampton. Anna held onto Karl's other hand, and Lars being weighed down with two suitcases, a valise, and several tote bags, walked behind his family.

Their friend Mr. Lindgren busied himself reading the gate numbers and train destinations. He determined that the train to Chicago, Illinois was loading at Gate 17 and he ushered the Persson family in that direction. Passengers were already forming lines to board the train. Now it was time for Harry Lindgren and the Persson family to go their separate ways. Lars set down the suitcases and totes and eagerly shook Harry Lindgen's hand.

"Harry, I just can't find the right words to thank you for all your help with getting my family here to America," Lars said. "I hope that someday we'll see each other again."

"Well, Lars, it was my pleasure to do what I could," answered Harry. "And who knows, maybe someday we will meet again."

Having said their goodbyes, Harry turned from the family and headed to Gate 21 where he would board a train taking him to Boston.

The line of passengers to Chicago moved along quickly and soon the Perssons would be ready to climb up the steps and enter the train. A black porter was standing by the train and when he noticed Anna struggling to climb the big step onto the train, he gently picked her up and placed her upwards into the doorway of the rail car. As soon as Anna noticed he looked different, she broke out screaming in fear. She had never before seen a black man and was terribly frightened of him. Quickly Karin mounted the steps and moved next to Anna calming her down. The family found their seats and soon the train was leaving the New Jersey terminal.

They arrived in Chicago late the following afternoon and were met by Lars' brother, Sander, who lived about fifty miles away. Sander took them to a hotel where they stayed overnight. Early the next morning, they once again boarded another train. Sander rode with them until the train reached the small town where he lived. Handshakes and loving embraces were exchanged before the Persson family continued along their journey, facing the unknown by themselves.

The flat prairies of Illinois gave way to Wisconsin dairy lands, then crossing the Mississippi River, a Sweden-like Minnesota emerged as the train moved along to the west. The changing scenes were scarcely noticed by the Perssons though. All were nearly exhausted from their long, long journey and they spent most of this train time dozing. This leg of the trip involved stops at every town along the way, or so it seemed. The hours droned by as the family alternately slept and awoke to the sound of the train whistle announcing the arrival at each depot. During the first several stops Anna asked, "Is this our new home?" only to be disappointed by Lars reply, "Not yet, liten flicka."

At six o'clock the next morning, the train at last pulled to a stop in Mankato, Minnesota. Here the weary family was directed to yet another train that would carry them the remaining ten miles to St. Peter.

Karl spoke up as they were climbing aboard the last train saying, "Poppa, let's just stay here. I can't go any farther!" "Yes, son, I know you're tired, but we must go just a little farther. Uncle Otto will be waiting to see us," Lars continued.

Less than an hour later the final train ride was over and there at the station, as Lars had promised, stood Uncle Otto. The train had scarcely drawn to a stop when Otto ran to meet Lars and his family as they made their way down the steps.

"Välkommen, välkommen," he cried excitedly to the family. "Look at this fine little sailor," he said as he reached to take the smiling baby from Karin's tired arms. "Hello little man. Välkommen to America!"

CHAPTER 3:

SETTLING IN

By the time the Perssons reached St. Peter, they were nearly exhausted and well past hungry. Uncle Otto had made arrangements to borrow Mr. Larson's automobile to bring them from the depot, and the shiny black vehicle was parked where they could see it as they left the train. Karin and the children climbed into the back seat, Anna on one side of Karin, Karl on the other and Bill, still smiling and looking about, perched on his mother's lap. Even though the children had never before been in an automobile; they were much too tired to be excited by this new experience. Lars took the front seat by his brother and after a five-mile ride, they reached the farm home of Uncle Carl and Aunt Gerda Johnson.

Lars' and Otto's sister Gerda and her husband Carl had been in America for several years and were already settled into new surroundings and customs. By a strange coincidence, the Persson family arrived on Thanksgiving Day and Gerda, in recognition of this American holiday, had prepared a fine dinner of roast turkey, dressing, mashed potatoes and homemade pies. Lars and Karin could hardly believe the feast that was set before them. It was months later when they finally realized that this fine meal was not only to welcome them, it was prepared to celebrate Thanksgiving.

Once the final plate and cup had been washed and put away, the youngsters began amusing themselves; chasing about the kitchen and entertaining each other as children do. The grownups found chairs in the parlor while the smallest cousins played contentedly on a blanket that was spread on the floor in front of the settee. News of their mutual Persson family in Sweden was exchanged and plans were made for the weeks to come.

Much too soon, it was time to load the family into the car once again, this time with a jar of milk and bowls of food which Gerda so graciously offered them for their first few meals in their new home. A short ride later they arrived at the farmhouse that would become their home on the property of Mr. Larson.

The house was sparsely furnished with two beds, a table with four chairs, a small wooden cupboard and a large wood burning kitchen range. Otto had layed wood in the stove early that morning and soon a comforting fire radiated heat into the kitchen.

"Here you are. All the comforts of home," he stated. "Tack så mycket," Karin quickly answered, grateful to at last see what would be their new American home. Otto accepted her words of thanks and replied, "we'll get your trunks to you first thing in the morning." Then with one more wave of his hand he stepped out of the door and left the tired family to find their way to bed.

Across the kitchen, a doorway led into a bedroom where two large beds invited the weary family to come and rest. A small table stood between the beds and eight pegs on the opposite wall would serve as a closet. Within minutes of Otto's departure, Karl and Anna climbed into bed. Karin nursed her baby son once more before settling down with him, lying next to Anna, who was already sleeping. Lars banked the fire for the evening, and soon contented sounds of the sleeping family filled the small house.

It was well past seven o'clock the next morning before anyone stirred. Lars awoke first and got up to refill the stove with wood from the wood box that stood by the kitchen door. The blaze took quickly and in no time, welcoming heat from the stove chased the November chill from the house.

The baby was next to open sleepy eyes to see his mother and sister still lost in their dreams on either side of him. Lars reached to pick him up before his morning cries might wake Anna.

"Well, there Billy Boy. What do you think of your new home?" Lars asked his little son. The baby squirmed against his wet "nappies" in uncomfortable reply.

"Just a minute, son. Poppa will find some dry things," he said. Crossing the room, Lars found the valise with the baby's clothing and soon had the little boy changed and dressed.

"It'll be up to your mother to give you breakfast, son," he spoke to the baby. Bill had found his thumb and was vigorously sucking on it, but this handily found consolation was not satisfying his hunger.

Karin was next to open her eyes. The sounds of the baby noisily smacking had stirred her from sleep. Quickly she arose, stepped into her shoes, threw on her coat and hurriedly made her way "down the path" and back once more to the warmth of the kitchen.

"Goodness, but it's cold out there today," she said to Lars. "I'll take the baby just as soon as I warm my hands again," she said as she held her hands near the stove. By now Bill had been patient long enough and his hungry wails filled the room. "Well, listen to that," Lars exclaimed, "he's really found his American appetite hasn't he!"

Soon Karl and Anna awoke and joined their parents at the table. Karin rose from her chair and laid her contentedly full baby son back down on the bed. Then she turned to the kitchen cupboard to find an enameled saucepan and the box of oatmeal that Otto had included when he opened the house in preparation for his brother's family.

"Otto has been so thoughtful by leaving this for our first breakfast in our new home," she thankfully offered.

"When he comes by this morning, to take me to town to pick up the trunks, we'll stop by the store for more supplies," Lars said to Karin.

The oatmeal had scarcely begun to bubble in the pan when a knock came at the door. Lars rose from his chair to answer, and opening the door, found Otto there with bag of groceries.

"Well, good morning," Otto offered to the family. "It looks like breakfast is started. I've brought along a loaf of bread. And there are some vegetables from Mr. Larson. He said they had more than enough for their family in the root cellar. I thought you would need some coffee beans for your morning coffee. There should be a grinder and coffeepot around here someplace."

Quickly bowls and cups were added on the table and soon everyone sat down to enjoy breakfast.

"I brought the team and wagon this morning so we could pick up your things from the train station, Lars," Otto told his brother." Mr. Larson said you could wait until later today to come by his house and talk to him. From the looks of it, it will take both of us to load those trunks of yours," he continued. "Did you bring all or just part of Sköne with you?" he teased.

Smiling silently at his brother's humor, Lars stood up from the table, gathered the empty bowls, and placed them in the enameled dishpan full of water that was sitting in the wall-hung sink. Retrieving his coat and cap from the wall hook, he began putting them on saying to Karin, "What else do we need to get in town?"

Karin got up from the table and began to place the coffee beans and oatmeal box back into the cupboard. "Well, let me think for a minute," she began. "Otto has brought potatoes and carrots, some dried beans, corn meal and flour. I could make a big pot of soup or stew if you brought home a soup bone or a few pieces of ham. Maybe a few onions also, and we do have the food that Gerda sent home with us."

Otto and Lars stepped out of the door into the morning chill, then Lars called back to his family, "We'll be back just as soon as we can. Hopefully by noon, but maybe a bit later, depending on how Otto's team works with their load."

"Don't you worry, Karin," Otto quickly called back to his sister-in-law. "These fine beasts will pull anything from the plow to a wagon full of rock. We'll be home again by noon if I know them," he said.

Karl and Anna stood looking out the kitchen window as the horses and men made their way down the short lane to the main road. They watched as long as they could see the wagon, then turned back into the room where their mother was busily wiping the table before she started to wash the dishes.

"Go quietly into the bedroom and find the suitcases," Karin directed. "You can find some clothes to wear can't you?" she asked. Soon the children returned to the kitchen, dressed and ready for the day. Karin bent to Anna and fastened the buttons that Anna's small fingers could not manage. Karl was carrying a small metal truck that Mr. Lindgren had given him in New York just before they boarded the train for the trek West. Anna was busying herself with "Inga", happily chatting to the doll and telling her all about their new home.

As soon as the kitchen was in order again, Karin returned to the bedroom to retrieve a bright-eyed Bill who was looking about his new surroundings as he lay on the bed. Picking up the baby, she carried him to the kitchen where she placed him on the rag rug in front of the cupboard. "Anna, do you know where that little red ball is? You remember, the one that Bill played with on the boat?" she questioned.

Quickly the little girl went to the bedroom and retrieved the ball from one of the suitcases. Running back into the kitchen, she handed the ball to the smiling baby. Karin gazed about the kitchen, taking in the happy childhood noises of her children at play in their new home.

"Well, already we are settling in," she thought to herself. "I wonder what the folks back home in Borrby are doing today?"

CHAPTER 4:

CHILDHOOD DAYS

Uncle Otto and Aunt Marlene Persson lived just a few miles from Lars and Karin. Once the new immigrants had settled into their home, Otto frequently came by to see how they were doing. Many times Lars commented to Karin that he didn't know what they would have done without all the help that came from his brother. Sometimes the help was food; a few potatoes or pork from the last hog butchered. Other times it was merely the warmth of a short, spontaneous visit as Otto passed by the farm.

Uncle Otto's visits often included small gifts for each of the children, usually a few pieces of candy. Bill had been his uncle's favorite from the time Otto first saw the baby when he met Lars' family at the train depot. The little boy would eagerly toddle to greet his uncle, anticipating a sweet treat. And while Otto saw to it that each of the children got their share; everyone could see that his main affection was for the baby of the family, little Bill.

The days of Bill's infancy had passed in what seemed a blink of an eye. He advanced through all the steps of babyhood; learning to sit, to crawl, to stand and finally to walk. He was just past his second birthday when another son came to join the Persson family.

It was early evening of the June day when the new baby had arrived, that Uncle Otto drove into the farmyard in his latest car, a black Model T. Otto didn't seem to keep the same car long enough to put wear on the tires and he somehow managed to drive something newer and better each time he made a trade. Otto loved to joke that "Old Henry Ford himself is surely grateful that I'm alive to keep him going."

After slowing his Model T to a halt, Otto eased himself out of the car, enjoying the hard sound of metal against metal as he solidly closed the car door. With a final pat to "T's" shiny black side, he turned and walked into the house.

"Well, what have we here," he called out to Lars who was busy ladling out soup to the three children sitting at their supper table. "Are you the cook now?" he teased.

"Where is your mother?" he questioned the children. Eagerly little Bill answered, "Baby." Anna quickly added, "We have a new brother. His name will be John." Karl remained quiet, more intent on eating his supper than responding to Otto.

Quickly Otto turned from the kitchen and poked his head into the bedroom where he could see Karin asleep in bed, holding a tiny blanketed form, and just as quickly he turned back to Lars and the children in the kitchen.

"So, you have a fine new son. Congratulations," he said as he slapped Lars on the back. Soon he opened a small package taken from his pocket and produced the anticipated sweets for the children.

"Finish your supper first," Lars ordered. "There will be time enough for sweets later."

"Your father is right," Otto agreed. "The soup comes first."

Then with just a few more minutes of conversation, Otto opened the kitchen door and stepped across the porch and down the steps to his waiting vehicle. With a loud starting clang of the engine, he was out of the farmyard and chugging down the road towards his home.

The family quickly adjusted to a new baby in the house, each doing what they could to help with added chores. Karl was to keep the kindling and wood box full. Anna did her five year old best to help also. She learned to pull a chair up to the table and soon was able to handle washing and drying dishes with Karin's supervision. Bill's job was that he remain the same happy, smiling child that he had always been. Somehow he didn't even mind that caring for the new baby took his mother's time away from him. He managed to stay as close to Karin as he could though, snuggling in the new rocking chair with her as she nursed little John.

The greatest adjustment fell to Lars and Karin as they worked their way through Karin's "sad times" after the birth of their newest baby. Her tears began shortly after John was born and several months passed before they stopped again. She was able to function as usual in the everyday care of her house and family, and she tried never to show her sadness in front of the children. But many nights Lars held her close as they lay in bed, stroking her head and lovingly assuring her that things would be all right as she sobbed into her pillow.

Soon the summer passed, and September was upon them. Karl would be going into the second grade. He secretly hoped that this year he would be allowed to drive the horse and buckboard by himself to school, but Lars cautioned that he was still too young for that.

More summers and more Septembers came and went, and in the ordinary passage of everyday life, the years slipped by. Bill celebrated his sixth birthday in March of 1925 and that September he would join his siblings for the start of the school year. He had been familiar with the District Number 32 School as long as he could remember. He went with his parents and siblings to various school picnics and Christmas parties. He listened carefully as Karl and Anna read from their readers each evening after supper. He marveled as Karl talked about geography class. Where were all those fascinating places? Was the ocean really so vast? He could scarcely wait to go to school and learn about everything for himself.

Bill was up early for his first day of school. He didn't have a new shirt to wear but Karin had deftly mended an old one of Karl's and Bill thought it looked as good as new. Anna and Karl gathered their pencils and tablets and soon everyone was ready to load into the buckboard for the ride to school. Karl would be twelve this year and had been responsible for getting himself and Anna to school for the past two years.

"Come on, little brother," Karl yelled into the kitchen where Karin was brushing Bill's hair to submission.

"We don't want to be late on the first day. All the good seats will be taken," he teased. Seeing Bill's worried face, Karin quickly countered, "Don't you be concerned, little son. You will be able to find a place right up in the first row."

Lydia Swenson was the teacher again this year. She had completed eight grades at District 32, then gone on to some months of "normal" training in Mankato. Two years ago at age at seventeen, she began teaching at District 32. Now she was back for another term. Although Lydia stood a strong five feet four inches, several of the eighth grade boys had grown to be taller than she was. Very soon they learned that she would not be intimidated by anything or anyone. She became an excellent teacher, long remembered at District 32.

Karl and Anna remembered Miss Swenson from previous years at school and she recognized the Persson children also. Uncle Otto's children and Aunt Gerda Johnson's children also attended this same country school. Bill was very happy to see the familiar faces of his cousins when he arrived at the schoolhouse, and soon he took his seat with two other students starting the first grade. The happy days in first grade elapsed in no time, each one seemingly to increase Bill's curiosity to learn and enjoy the wonder of the world that he lived in.

When school started the following year, it was a day that the Persson family wouldn't soon forget. The children were up much before they needed to be, eager and ready for school when a car drove into the yard, and was it a beauty! The youngsters raced to the window to see who was driving this fancy automobile. The 1926 Chevy touring car had a yellow body and tan fabric top. The wooden spoke wheels had white sidewall tires and in case the Perssons hadn't seen the car drive in, the loud "ah-ooga" of the horn soon announced an important presence.

The door opened and out stepped Uncle Otto, dressed in his finest. He was wearing a dark suit, complete with spats over his shoes. The children hardly recognized him, dressed as he was.

"Well, hello there, brother," Lars called from the porch. "You're certainly looking prosperous."

"Ya, ya. Times are good," Otto answered without further elaboration.

"How about I give you a ride to school today?" he said to the children.

Karl, Anna and Bill quickly bounded down the steps and joined Otto's son and daughter in the car. In no time they were speeding down the road towards District 32.

As soon as the dust in the yard had settled, Lars and Karin headed back into their house. "I'm worried about Otto," Lars began. "Where does he get the money to buy a fancy automobile like that? I wonder if he's doing more than making a quart or two for himself these days," Lars added.

Prohibition had changed a lot of people from simple, hardworking men to slick dealers out for the fast dollar. Could it be true that his brother had become one of them? Without saying it aloud, Lars suspected that Otto had advanced from making homebrew just for himself, to the more dangerous part of "moonshining", delivery of the product. This was where lots of big money could be made and would explain how Otto was able to afford the fine cars that he drove.

The speculation came to bare truth a few months later when Otto was arrested and sentenced to three months at the county jail in Gaylord. As difficult as the shame of having a sibling incarcerated might be, Lars saw to it that his family went to visit Uncle Otto. He had never forgotten Otto's kindness to his family and felt the least they could do for Otto in this trouble, was to visit him in jail.

Once a week the children would be loaded into the old Model T for the twenty-some mile trip to Gaylord where they were able to see Uncle Otto for an hour or so in the large visiting area at the jailhouse. The first trip was exciting and all were anxious to go. But by the fourth visit, Bill had had enough. "Why do we have to keep coming," he complained. "I'm tired of sitting in jail every Sunday."

The words from the seven-year-old boy were enough to curtail the visits. From then on Uncle Otto served his sentence without any more visits from Bill and his siblings. Lars would still make an occasional visit by himself but he excused the rest of his family from the trip.

Sadly, the jail sentence was not the end of Otto's criminal involvement. Just a few years later he was involved in a bank robbery. He was still driving his fancy yellow Chevrolet and was quickly spotted as he and his cohorts sped away from the bank. This time he would be sent to State Prison. Otto's family life and marriage soon fell apart, the effects rippling through all the Persson family.

Lars, more than anyone, felt the aftermath of his brother's criminality. He was still trying to recover from the news that had come to him in April of 1925. Far-Mor Gertrude had written to inform him that his youngest brother Karl had been lost in a ship accident. Karl was only sixteen at the time and was working on a freighter, the Orion. This ship was carrying cement from Limhamn to Luleå when it collided with another ship in dense fog. Karl was just about to be rescued, when the Orion gave a sudden lurch and he was lost into the ocean.

Although there was fourteen years difference in age between Lars and Karl, they had enjoyed a special bond as brothers. Karl was ten years old when Lars and his family left Sweden and the picture of a tearful young brother sadly saying goodbye, never left his memory. For many years Lars quietly mourned the loss of this youthful sailor. When the news of Otto's prison sentence reached him, his sadness only deepened. He did what he could to help Marlene and Otto's children work through their separation from Otto, but it somehow it never was quite enough and the families drifted apart.

Of course Bill, even at this young age, felt the detachment from his Uncle Otto. Regardless of his impatience at "sitting in jail every Sunday", he still deeply loved Otto. He missed Otto's impromptu visits, the spontaneous treats for all, and the thrill of a wild swing through the air when Otto would swoop him upwards. The little metal sailor bank that Otto had brought him on his last birthday would become even more precious to him than when he first received it. Bill kept the bank on the floor under his bed and on those rare occasions when a penny crossed his fingers, he'd remember Uncle Otto as he plunked a coin into the bank.

There were happy, exciting days for the Perssons during these years as well as the ones marked by sadness and disappointments. Lars became a citizen of the United States in 1926 and Karin followed his lead in 1927, just a few months before a new child came to join the family.

Little Jana Rose was born in August of 1927 and the Persson household quickly expanded to make room for their latest addition. Anna was delighted to have a baby sister to play with and care for. Bill and John found themselves enchanted by baby smiles and happy baby sounds from the newest Persson. Even Karl, who was just entering his teenage years, could not resist talking to Jana whenever he passed by the little one as she lay on her blanket.

With a lot of hard work and determination, Lars had managed to pay off the last of the immigration loan and began adding farm equipment and livestock to the family assets. He had rented land for a number of years and began purchasing used equipment as finances allowed. Four head of horses and seventeen head of cattle comprised the livestock the Perssons owned. The children had been especially delighted when Lars bought a bobsled. In their adult years, the memories of winter rides to Christmas church services, all cuddled under a buffalo robe, were a special part of childhood stories they loved to retell. The usual farm menagerie of dogs, cats, chickens and ducks was also fondly remembered.

Bill was eleven years old when he decided that he would take over planting and caring for the family garden. Karin was delighted with his offer, since keeping up with the care of five children and a house, took nearly all of her time. It would be a great help to have someone take care of a garden.

As soon as the seed catalog arrived in late January, Bill pored over the pages, making plans for the garden. Each evening after he had completed his homework, he sat at the kitchen table, turning the pages of the catalog back and forth, planning and revising the list of the seeds that he wished to order.

"We'll need peas and corn. I'm going to order carrots, cabbage, tomatoes and beans too," he announced to his mother one evening. "Come look at this page. They show seed peanuts to plant. Can I try some of these too?" he asked.

Lars glanced up from reading the latest letter from Sweden to answer him, "What makes you think that peanuts will grow in Minnesota?"

"Well, I guess I won't know if I don't try," was the answer and since that seemed a reasonable reply, Lars agreed that Bill could also add peanuts to the list of seed that would be ordered. That same evening from the back of the well-thumbed booklet, Bill filled out the order blank for the seeds. "I'll get a money order in town tomorrow and mail this then," Lars said. "The seeds should come by the first of March in time for you to start the cabbage and tomatoes inside."

In mid October of that year as Bill raked the last of the vines and dried leaves from the garden, he again enjoyed thinking about his unusual garden crop. By now the gardens in the county were stripped clean of the various vegetables that had fed families all that summer. Judging by the many rows of shiny glass jars full of colorful corn, beans, tomatoes, and beets that sat on groaning cellar shelves, the vegetable crops would continue to feed families during the winter. But only one of the gardens could boast of producing peanuts! Bill had proven his point. Peanuts could grow in Minnesota!

When the school year began in the fall of 1930, Miss Swenson was not there to greet the students. She had married a young man from the neighborhood in late June. Oscar Olson and his family lived on a farm, just to the west of the Persson place and he had been a regular part of the crews that came to help put up hay or harvest wheat. Bill and his family knew Oscar well and were pleased that Miss Swenson would remain close by after her marriage, even though she was not allowed to continue teaching once she married.

Bill was hopeful that the new teacher, Miss Johnson, would be as warm and friendly as Miss Swenson had been. He truly loved going to school and from the time he started in first grade, he soaked up all the knowledge that he could. He listened in as each grade had their lessons and so as he advanced through the grades himself, he came into each already somewhat knowledgeable of what was being taught at a particular time. Miss Johnson proved herself to be as proficient as Miss Swenson, and at the same time being just as well loved by her students. Bill and the rest of the students happily settled into the new school year.

The pages on the calendar turned quickly and before anyone could think about it, summer vacation rolled around again. May of 1931 brought another daughter to join the Persson household. This new baby girl, Lorraine, brought the number of living children to six, three girls and three boys, but not all lived at home anymore. Karl had been working as a hired man since leaving school in mid 1928 when he felt earning money was more valuable to him than struggling to learn to find the contents of a cube or whether "occasional" was spelled with one "s" or two.

Anna chose to continue her education past eighth grade and was living with a family in St. Peter, working to pay her room and board with them in her free time after school and on weekends. Bill, John, Jana and the new baby Lorraine constituted the siblings living at the Persson home.

At the age of thirteen, Bill had become the right hand man for his father. He and Lars worked side-by-side putting in the crops and getting them out again. The workload was increased when Karl left, but Bill did his best to keep up and at the same time continue his education. He particularly loved taking care of the horses. Barney and Maude were a team of matched dray horses that Lars had purchased from his brother just after Otto bought his first car. They were fine, strong animals that willingly pulled the plow or trotted contently in front of the buggy.

On a warm June morning when Jana was five, Bill hitched up Barney and Maude. He intended to make a trip into Norseland, a small town just a few miles from the farm where the Persson's lived. Karin had asked Bill to go into town for the groceries she needed.

Jana was sitting on a large stump of wood in the barnyard watching him work with the harness.

"Would you like to ride along to town with me?" Bill asked his little sister. In a flash she ran to the house to tell her mother she was going with Bill. Running back to the barnyard, she climbed into the buggy and Bill clicked a "giddy-up" to the eager horses.

The trip to town was uneventful, passing quickly as Bill sang all the songs that he could think of and Jana joined in with the words that she knew. The groceries were purchased, loaded into the buggy and the return trip begun.

On the way home, Bill drove the buggy through a wooded patch of ground, a "short-cut" he explained to Jana. All at once, something spooked the horses. They reared in fright and began to gallop along as Bill struggled to regain control. As they raced along, the buggy wheel came loose from the rim and rolled ahead of them along the wooded drive. Bill managed to pull the horses to a stop and only then he and Jana began laughing at the sight of the buggy wheel rolling ahead of them. Once the wheel was reattached, the trip resumed but both Bill and Jana were still laughing as they turned down the lane towards home.

On a lazy Sunday afternoon several months after the runaway adventure, Bill tore a page from the calendar, intending to write a note on it to his sister Anna. Anna had not been able to come home from her job in town for a number of weeks and he missed her. He wandered out to the sulky plow, at rest beside the barn, and sat down on the hard metal seat to begin his composition.

The attraction he had towards the ocean surfaced in his writing that day. Much later in his life he would find himself writing yet another letter; this time thinking about his Minnesota home as he sat on a different seat; the hard hot metal of a Navy destroyer as they cruised thousands of miles from all that was familiar.

To Anna
The Fisherman That Didn't Return

I

A fisherman lived by the side of the sea
Alone with his wife and family of three
But he'll greet them no more by
That little cottage door
For he rests beneath the green sea foam.

II

When one night he did not return
A very sad story they were to learn
The wind raged outside

While the white sea gulls cried
And his boat was upset in the storm.
III
For his pillow he has seaweed
For his blanket he has foam
The dark waters do surround him
But he'll greet them no more
By that little cottage door
For he sleeps beneath the green sea foam.

(Written by Billie as he sat musing on the sulky plow. Age 13 years)

Once again the months slipped by and September of 1932 saw Bill starting eighth grade. Only two boys remained in eighth grade that year, most having decided to quit school and find what work they could to help their families at home. Miss Johnson was there to greet the students and those who knew her were pleased that she would be their teacher at least one more time. The school year began humming along. The old oak tree in front of the school once again witnessed lessons that were recited, songs that were sung and the happy sounds of children at play during recess.

Bill's eighth grade notebook became filled with many important lessons to him that year; 5 ½ yards = 1 rod, 128 cubic feet =1 cord of wood or stone, 70 pounds =1 bushel of corn, and of course, pages and pages of spelling words. All the information became invaluable whether one chose to stay on the farm or set his sights on something else.

Life continued on at home on the Persson farm, this family like so many others of the day, struggling through hard times. The Great Depression had begun in 1929 and it would seem that bare necessities had turned into luxuries. It became harder and harder for men to provide food, clothing and shelter for their families. Farm families had an advantage in that it was somewhat easier to feed themselves, but finding an extra dollar for anything else was difficult, and most times impossible. Often that year Bill considered joining his friends and his brother Karl, who had quit school at Bill's age. Each time he approached Lars for advice on this, Lars would say, "Son, stay in school and get what education you can. You can work the rest of your life." Bill took his father's advice and was one of two boy graduates in the eighth grade class of 1933.

CHAPTER 5:

INTO THE
WORKING WORLD

The transition from being a schoolboy of fourteen to a hired hand of fourteen was a common experience to most young farm boys living in the 1930's. Sometimes even younger boys left school and found themselves taking their place in the long lines of people looking for work. Bill had known what hard work was from the time he was able to drive a team, milk a cow or put up hay. During these years on the farm, there was no question that children would help as they could with various chores. All hands, regardless of their size, were needed to put in the crops, get them out again, tend livestock and so forth. It wasn't a matter of just being a good child and lending assistance. It was essential that everyone worked so that the family was able to feed themselves and to prepare the crops for market. Everyone was given chores according to their age and ability. The main difference was in working for pay for someone else or working at home just to ease the physical burden on the head of the household, without expected compensation, other than room and board.

While the prospect of getting paid for one's labor was appealing, work as a hired hand was not always easy to come by during the Depression Days. Often young men would hire out for a few weeks and if they were lucky, this tenure could turn into months. Then it was back home again, helping there while at the same time continuing their search for the possibilities of another job on a different farm, going from place to place in the hope of bettering one's pay and position.

During the summer of 1933, Bill helped various farmers with haying while he remained living at home. Once the first crop of hay was harvested, he helped Lars on the family farm. The next crop to mature was wheat. The ripened wheat was swathed and stacked into golden shocks to dry before it was time for the threshing crew to arrive. In mid July, the threshing crew began their rounds through the area, proceeding from farm to farm until everyone's wheat crop had been threshed.

Bill and his friend Fred Schmidt, worked side by side feeding the shocks into the thresher where grain was separated from stalk. One of the farms where the crew worked, was owned by Ed Swanson. It so happened that Mr. Swanson's hired man had left to return to his home in Wisconsin and Mr. Swanson approached Bill about coming to work as his hired man. Ed had observed Bill as they went from farm to farm with the threshers, and he could tell that Bill was a tireless worker. He saw that as young as Bill was, he pulled his own weight and was not one to slack off and leave the harder jobs to somebody else.

"Bill, would you like to come to work for me full time?" Mr. Swanson questioned as the wheat harvesting crew finished their noon meal.

Bill didn't pause long enough to swallow as he quickly answered, "Yes, sir. I would. When can I start?" he asked.

"Well, my man Francis has already gone, so you could come Sunday night. You'll have his room upstairs and we promise to feed you good too! You can start early on Monday morning," Mr. Swanson went on. The wages offered to the young boy were more than fair, and an exuberant Bill left the Swanson place that day with exciting news to share at home. He had a full time job!

Once the days' work of harvesting was complete, Bill hopped in Fred Schmidt's dilapidated pickup truck for the seven-mile ride home. He and Fred rode without talking. Even if they had wanted to converse, they would have to shout at each other to be heard above the noise of the lumbering old vehicle. Instead, Bill spent the travel time pondering his new- found fortune. In his mind he was already amassing great sums of money. He was purchasing new clothes, giving a few dollars to Lars to help at home, buying a bicycle. Life was looking up!

Karin prepared fried chicken for supper that evening. Bill had told her when he left in the morning that today was his last day with the crew at Swanson's. She decided that a nice supper would be a way to commemorate the end of the wheat harvest season. For good measure, she had baked an apple pie, Bill's favorite.

Jana was just putting the plates on the table when Bill bounded into the house all excited with his good news of the day.

"Mom, I got a job!" he excitedly told his mother. Karin turned from the cooking to face her son, smiling a welcome home as she listened to his excited words. "Did you hear me?" he persisted. "I got a job!"

"Well, congratulations, son," she answered. "That's wonderful news. Tell me about it," she went on.

Once the family had gathered around the table and began their supper, Bill told them of the opportunity that came to him that day from Mr. Swanson. All were pleased to share his good news. The littlest family member, Lorraine, also joined in the excitement, clapping her hands and smiling as the family laughed and talked together.

The following Sunday afternoon, Bill busied himself packing a small valise with his clothing. He also put in several small notebooks left over from his school years. During the past year, Bill had started keeping a diary. Now he was anxious to record the ordinary and the not so ordinary events that surely would come along with this change in his life. Mr. Swanson came by for him about 5:00 in the evening. Karin and Lars watched their young son climb into Mr. Swanson's big truck and they waved their anxious goodbyes as the truck turned down the lane.

"It seems just yesterday when he was a baby," Karin sadly commented. "Ya, the years went by fast, didn't they," replied Lars. Both had begun missing their son as soon as he announced the news of his first full time job.

The miles between the Persson place and Mr. Swanson's farm, passed with pleasant conversation between Bill and Mr. Swanson. Ed explained to Bill just what his everyday duties would be, what time the day began at the Swanson's, and that he was expected to attend church with the family on those Sundays he remained with them.

The Swanson farm was one of the largest in the area. The long lane leading in was lined on both sides with evergreen trees and the large two-story house had a porch wrapped around three sides. A young boy of about nine and his fourteen- year old sister sat in rocking chairs on the front porch waiting for their father to return with the new hired man. As soon as she heard the truck turn into the lane, Mrs. Swanson did a final check on the meat and vegetables roasting slowly in the oven, then she stepped onto the porch to join the children.

"Hello, there young Master William," she called out as Bill stepped from the truck. "Come right in. This is our son, Elmer." She went on to introduce Rosemarie who smiled a greeting. "Elmer will show you where your room is before we have supper. I hope you like roast beef and vegetables," she continued.

Bill and Elmer entered the house through the front door and proceeded up the stairs. Elmer led the way down the upstairs hallway, to the last room on the left. "This is your room, William," Elmer said. "The bathroom is across the hall. My room is next to yours and my sister Rosemarie has the first one at the top of the stairs."

Bill stepped into the room and set his battered valise on the floor by the bed. "You might want to wash up before supper," Elmer continued. "Come down whenever you're finished."

Bill stood in the room, trying to take in the glorious size and beauty of the Swanson house. It was a far cry from the Persson place, which was a simple one-story house that had bedrooms haphazardly added on as the size of the family increased. And wonder of wonders-there was even a bathroom! He could only imagine the luxurious feel of sitting in a real bathtub, not the galvanized washtub he used at home. He washed his hands, and then went downstairs to join Elmer and Rosemarie on the front porch while all waited for Mr. Swanson to finish evening chores.

Soon Mr. Swanson returned to the house, changed out of his work clothing, and all proceeded to the large dining room for their meal. Mrs. Swanson showed Bill to a place at the table, and the Sunday evening meal began.

"Well, William, did you find the room to your liking," Mr. Swanson questioned. "Yes sir, I certainly did," Bill answered. "And I'd like you to call me Bill." Mr. Swanson quickly replied that he could be called "Ed" and that Mrs. Swanson was "Helen."

Rosemarie tittered aloud at the conversation but quickly regained her composure after a scathing glance from her mother.

As soon as the meal was over, Mr. Swanson took Bill into the living room and proceeded to lay out his plans for what was to be done the following week and just what Bill would be expected to do. It wasn't long before the grandfather clock in the hall chimed eight times.

"You'll probably want to turn in early tonight," Mr. Swanson said. "I'd like to get started on the fence repair just as soon as we finish the milking. Those cows of mine start bawling about 5:30 in the morning so we should be in the barn by 6:00 for chores."

Mr. Swanson wished everyone good night and Bill, Elmer and Rosemarie climbed the stairs to their bedrooms. Ed and Helen retired to their bedroom just off of the dining room and the house-hold settled into peaceful nighttime silence.

Bill lay in bed gazing out the window into the starry August night. He knew that he should try to get to sleep. Morning would come early and there was lots of work to get done as Mr. Swanson had explained. Yet he couldn't help being excited about this whole new adventure. This bedroom was bigger than any room he had ever slept in and having a bed to himself was new to him also. From early childhood on, he had to share a bed with either Karl or John. He almost missed the sounds of a sleeping brother by his side, but soon the luxury of space to himself and the peaceful quietness of the house led him to sleep.

At the Persson household, the gaiety of Saturday night's celebration dinner gave way to a somber Monday morning, minus Bill at their table. Without thinking, Karin had prepared the same amount of fried eggs as usual and the extra helpings sat on the platter to remind them of their absent member.

"Well, we can't just let these go to waste," John announced as he helped himself to the eggs prepared for his missing brother.

"I'll have to learn to cook for less now," Karin said. Then she quickly added as comfort to herself and her family, "He'll be able to have a day at home in about two weeks. Mr. Swanson said so." The five remaining Perssons finished breakfast in silence.

The workday at the Swanson place had begun early as Ed had said. He was already in the barn when Bill walked in at 5:45. "Good morning, Bill," Ed cheerfully said. "How did you sleep?"

"Just fine, Mr. Swanson, I mean "Ed", Bill answered. "It was kind of strange without anybody in the room with me though." Ed chuckled aloud, then went on with leading the cows into their respective stanchions to begin the milking. Soon he and Bill had finished up the last cow and it was time to go back into the house to eat the morning meal.

That evening, a very tired Bill climbed the stairs to his room. He got out his notebook and added a few words to his diary. "Learned the milking routine," "fixed fences," "played catch with Elmer after supper for a while," were the entries made on that day.

When Bill began keeping a diary, he had started with a description of himself at the time.

"Today I am about five feet seven inches. I weigh about 140 lbs. I am fourteen years, nine months, and eight days old. My hair is sandy, my eyes are grey. My hobbies are: collecting stamps, neglecting letter writing and going to town."

September, October and November on the Swanson place passed quickly. Bill had become almost like one of their family in just a few short weeks. Helen was especially fond of the young man who always called her "Ma'am" and never neglected to clear his dishes from the table after finishing his meal. Ed was certainly glad that he had taken on Bill as his hired hand. Bill never complained about additional chores given to him and always completed the job well over Ed's expectations. Elmer was simply delighted to have a "big brother", and Rosemarie was as smitten as only a young teen-aged girl could be.

About every two weeks or so, Mr. Swanson drove Bill home on Saturday afternoon for a short visit with his family. Lars would drive him back to the Swanson place on Sunday evening. The routine continued on through fall and into the winter. On his visits home, Bill could see that things were not going very well for Lars. It seemed the harder that Lars worked, the less he had to show for it. Karl and Bill gave their father a dollar or so when they could, but even this kind of help just wasn't enough. Some changes would have to be made.

Things went along better at the Swanson place. Bill often wondered why his father struggled so and Ed Swanson seemed to be doing just fine. Whether circumstances were different because of less debt, better management or just plain luck was an open question.

December of 1933 brought frigid temperatures to the Minnesota farm side, but measurable snow was not a part of the picture.

Helen didn't let the lack of snow deter her determination to "pro-claim Christmas" by decorating the house room by room. A large Christmas tree stood in front of the living room window, all strung with blue lights, and glistening with hundreds of tinsel strands dangling from the branches. Various Christmas decorations either hung from doorways or nestled on tables throughout the house.

Helen decided that they would celebrate their family Christmas with Bill the afternoon of December 24 before he went home to join the Perssons. She had prepared a sumptuous noontime feast of roast goose with all the trimmings. As soon as the kitchen was back in order, all returned to the living room to open their gifts. Each person in turn opened one package. Bill was pleased with the new flannel shirt he received but when he opened the package containing the harmonica, his face lit up in delight.

"Oh my goodness," he exclaimed. "I've always wanted to have one of these." "We'll expect music in the evenings now," Helen teased.

As soon as they had opened the last present, there was a knock on the front door. "I'll bet that's my dad here to pick me up," an excited Bill said. He got up from the chair and went to the door. Lars stood there all bundled up against the cold. "Come on in, Mr. Persson," Ed called out." Will you have a cup of hot cider with us?"

Lars stepped into the room and unwrapped the woolen muffler from his face. "That sounds mighty good, thank you. It's a cold one out there today."

While Lars and Ed enjoyed a cup of cider at the kitchen table, Bill quickly gathered his Christmas presents and bounded upstairs to gather some "church clothes" into his valise. Soon he was back downstairs and he and Lars were on the way home, calling "Merry Christmas" to all the Swansons as they left.

The ride home went quickly with Bill telling his father what had transpired since they were last together. Soon they pulled into the Persson farmyard and made their way into the house. Bill was pleased to see that Karl and Anna were already home for Christmas too. Wonderful smells of potato soup and homemade bread filled the house. The rest of Christmas Eve passed in the warm contentment of a family gathering together, enjoying their food, exchanging small gifts and sharing news of what had occurred since they were last all together. Much too quickly it was all over and it was time to end the day.

All the December snow that hadn't fallen earlier in the month fell collectively in the first hours of Christmas Day. Lars was the first to discover the wonderland of white as he opened the door to go out to the barn to begin morning chores. "It's a good thing I have the shovel handy here by door," he thought to himself as he began to clear a path to the barn. Once the animals were fed, he returned to the house again. He shook the snow from his coat and boots as he stepped into the lean-to on the back of the house. Karin was in the kitchen preparing breakfast and the sleepy household gathered in the kitchen one by one as they awakened.

Soon everyone was up, dressed and fed. "Are we going to church today," Karin asked. Karl quickly responded, "I'll go out and hitch Barney and Maude to the bob sled. Nobody's going any place in a car today." So it was decided that all would go, bundled up and wedged next to each other and on laps for the short sled ride to church. It was a scene that Currier and Ives would have been proud to picture!

All too soon the day was over and Bill returned once again to the Swanson's. He continued to write in his diary:

January	1	Cleaned out the barn, hauled wood
January	5	I had a tooth pulled
January	6	Had a swelled jaw. Helped a fellow out of the ditch at midnight
January	7	Found Rosemarie in my room today

January	9	Hauled wood
January	10	Helped set up new separator
January	23	Rosemarie still a pest

The ongoing flirtations from Rosemarie became a real trouble spot for Bill. He surely didn't want to offend the Swansons in any way, but still he didn't know how to tactfully tell Rosemarie to leave him alone. He tried to spend as much time as he could with Elmer after supper, helping the boy with his homework. Other evenings Bill passed his time by drawing in his notebook. He'd taught himself how to play the harmonica that he received for Christmas. Helen loved listening to his halting versions of "Red River Valley."

In the first few days of February, Lars reached the decision to sell off the stock and machinery. He had tried so hard to make a decent living and provide for his family, but no matter what he did; the income was never there. He could see so many other families struggling in the same way. At least once a month sale bills were posted when one more farmer decided to quit.

The auction was arranged to be held on Wednesday, February 28. All the Persson family gathered to watch as the cattle, horses and machinery were sold and taken away by new owners. When the bobsled was hauled off, the happy memories of their recent Christmas ride to church passed through the memory of all the family. But saddest of all, was watching the tears on John's young face as Barney and Maude were bought by Fred Schmidt's father.

Bill tried his best to console John by saying, "Hey, brother. The Schmidt's are fine people. They will take good care of Barney and Maude." John would not be comforted and hid by himself the rest of the day until the new owners had loaded and hauled their auction purchases away.

A few weeks later, Lars and his family moved to a different place. The new house was just outside of Le Sueur, so they were still living in the country. Lars considered himself very lucky to find a job in Le Sueur. He spent the rest of that winter at the "brick barn", a site owned by the local canning factory. His job was loading the silage sold to area farmers and also tending to the horses used by the factory. The prospect of getting a weekly paycheck, small that it was, made things so much better at home. John had quit school and he too was working as a hired hand. The three boys, Karl, Bill and John tried their best to save a few dollars. Whenever they could manage; they would slip a dollar or so to Lars to help at home. This was how the Perssons, like so many other families, found their way through difficult depression years.

Shortly after the Perssons moved to their new place, Bill decided to move on to another job with another set of circumstances. Karl had told him of a farmer in the Cleveland area who needed help and Bill made the arrangements to go to work for Lester Odegard. Much as he dreaded leaving the Swansons who had considered him as family, it was time for a change. The situation with Rosemarie's infatuation continued to get more intense on her part, and Bill needed a change. The prospect of higher wages plus getting away from a situation beyond his control, were the reasons that Bill found himself jumping at this new opportunity. Later when Helen wrote to Bill she mentioned "they all missed him so and that he would be welcome to come back at any time."

The transition from living with the Swanson family and moving to the Odegard farm about twenty miles to the south went pretty much without event. Lester and Marie Odegard were an older couple with grown children already gone from home. In this situation Bill really was the "hired man" and did not enjoy the same family relationship that he had at the Swansons. But he had made the decision to move, so now felt he must make the best of things. Much as he missed the camaraderie with Ed, Helen and Elmer, at least he would not have to deal with Rosemarie, her infatuation for him and the embarrassment this caused him.

Soon Bill settled into the routine of the Odegard farm. March in Minnesota often was a kind of a make-do month. Farmers busied themselves as they could, enduring a final March snowstorm, while at the same time welcoming the sight of the first springtime flower that braved the frigid air. Everyone counted the days until the last of cold and snow was gone for good. They filled their days caring for the livestock or chopping wood before it was time to get the fields ready to plant.

The morning of March 21 dawned to a chilly frostiness. Marie had fixed pancakes, a favorite breakfast of Bill's, and all had enjoyed the fluffy cakes drenched in maple syrup. While Lester was savoring his second cup of black coffee, he said to Bill, "Today I want you to chop some wood. We're going to need it to outlast this cold weather." Bill got up from the table, walked toward the enclosed back porch where his heavy coat and flop-eared hat were hanging. He called back into the room to Lester, "I'll get right to the chopping. I need to work off all those pancakes!"

Soon he was hard at work, swinging the axe deftly, splitting wood chunks into just the right size to load into the wood guzzling stoves in the Odegard home. After splitting a few large chunks, he laid the axe down and gathered the split wood into his arms and carried them to the wood stack where the new pieces were carefully arranged to insure that the pile would not slip or topple when the top pieces of wood were removed for use. He had been hard at this work about an hour when the accident happened. Later when he tried to reconstruct in his mind just what had happened, he could not. Whatever the distraction had been; a noise from the barn, the flutter of a hawk, a passing car on the road, he could not tell. He only knew that in the flash of a moment, a terrible pain began in his left thumb and in the next instant the work glove covering this hand oozed with warm blood. He could tell that his injury was serious and so he kept the glove on his hand as he hurried back to the house.

Marie had just finished sweeping the kitchen when Bill burst through the door. "I'm afraid I've had an accident," he began. Marie quickly pulled out a chair from the table and had him sit down.

"Let's take a look at this," she said as she pulled the wet kitchen towel from the rack. Carefully removing the glove to assess the damage, she could see the thumb looked to be nearly severed. Working quickly to try to stop the bleeding, she wrapped Bill's hand in the wet towel and directed him to stay in the chair. She ran out the back door, calling loudly to Lester who was working in the machine shed, "Come in here quickly. Bill's been hurt."

On the trip to town to the doctor's office Bill felt himself rising and falling on the edge of his pain. Whether Lester said one word to him, he did not know. The medical procedure involved in this accident was forever lost to memory also. Bill did remember that upon returning to the Odegard farm, Marie urged him to drink a warm cup of broth before he went into his room to lie down. The next few days passed in a painful blur as Bill alternately lay in his bed and walked as far as the kitchen to eat his meals. By the third day, however, he was getting restless, and so on that morning, he struggled into his work clothes and joined Lester in the early morning barn chores. March went out like a lion with a final blast of artic air, and when the April showers abated, it was time to begin to get ready for planting. Bill cheerfully worked with Lester as they got the plow edges sharpened and the noisy old tractor in running order. Now and then when he bumped the sore thumb, he was painfully reminded of the mishap, and long after the pain was gone, an ugly scar remained providing instant recall of the incident.

The visits back and forth between work and home had stretched from once every two weeks or so into five to six weeks. Bill resorted to writing home to his family to stay in touch, and now and then a letter would return to him. Karin had written asking how he was getting along with his sore hand, and in her latest note received in

May, mentioned that Jana had been sick for over a week with tonsillitis. It happened that on the first day of May, Jana and a friend made May baskets and enjoyed delivering them to three or four farms up and down the country road near their homes. As the girls were making their rounds, a sudden shower drenched them with chilling rain before they could return home again. As a result, Jana became seriously ill and had been confined to bed for ten days. Aspirin and bed rest was the only treatment available at the time.

Several weeks later Bill managed to get a ride home and enjoyed a much- needed visit with his family. By then Jana was feeling better but the doctor said that she must have her tonsils out as soon as possible. It was necessary to pay for this surgery beforehand and money was still very scarce in the Persson household.

On the first night of his visit home, Bill and Lars remained at the table while the dishes were cleared and the kitchen returned to order. With hesitancy in his voice Lars began, "Could I borrow a few dollars from you to help pay for Jana's operation?"

Without a second thought Bill answered, "I'll send over what I have as soon as I get back to Odegards. Watch the mail for a money order."

When he returned to the Odegard farm, Bill immediately went to his room and got out his metal sailor bank with saved coins and the cigar box that held $13.00 in dollar bills. Bill had been saving his hard-earned money to buy a bicycle, something he had dreamed of owning. But now after Lars' request for help, he didn't think twice about giving his money to aid in the payment for Jana's operation, all the while regretting that he couldn't offer more. The money was sent, the tonsils removed and the hope to own a bicycle delayed forever.

Summer and fall at Odegards passed pretty much uneventfully; crops were in, crops came out. Once in a while a trip to town changed the routine but more often than not, one day just mirrored the previous one. Bill continued making notations in his diary and varied "no news today" by entering jokes he heard, or the words to favorite songs played on the radio.

December arrived when no one was looking. On December 3, eight inches of snow fell to cover the countryside in a sparkling blanket of white. Then just a week before Christmas, another five inches were added to the rolling fields. The piles on each side of the roads grew higher and higher.

The day before Christmas, Bill was able to ride to Le Sueur with Lester and Marie who had gone there to buy Christmas gifts for their grandchildren. Bill tramped his way through the snowy sidewalks to Nichols' Variety Store. He had noticed the red sled in the window on a November trip to town and hoped the sled would still be there the next time he came back. It was, and he counted off and laid on the counter the $3.00 for his purchase. Once again the cigar box bank was empty but Bill couldn't think of a better way to spend his saved money. Mrs. Nichols tied a big red bow on top of the sled and Bill left the store with the sled in one hand, his small valise in the other.

As Bill started down the sidewalk, he spotted his friend Fred Schmidt, still driving the same old depilated truck, pull into a parking spot down the street from the variety store. When the engine ground to a halted silence, Bill approached the drivers' door as Fred stepped into the street.

"Hello, Fred. Merry Christmas," Bill said, glad to see his friend and hopeful that he might be able to catch a ride the mile or so from town to the Persson farm.

"Hi, buddy," Fred responded. "How's it going? Need a ride home," the questions tumbled out before Bill had a chance to ask the favor. Bill climbed into the truck with his bag and the present.

After Fred had finished his errand, the young men bounced along the gravel road yelling conversation above the noise of the truck. In no time they were at the Persson place, Bill jumped from the truck with a quick "thanks, pal" then hurried to the house. He propped the sled just outside the back door before going in.

"Merry Christmas. Merry Christmas!" he called into the kitchen. Quickly his two little sisters ran to greet him, embracing him with hugs and kisses. That evening, John and Anna were able to join the family to celebrate a joyous Christmas Eve together. On Christmas morning, Jana and Lorraine were delighted to discover the red sled by the Christmas tree. Soon they were spending many happy hours swooping down the hilly countryside, thanks to this special Christmas gift from their generous brother.

The piles of December 1934 snow remained well through January of 1935. There was no sign of the normal "January thaw" that winter and frigid temperatures continued, once reading thirty- six degrees below zero! Man and beast struggled alike against the cold. Bill grew accustomed to rising from his bed early in the morning, pulling on every available item of heavy clothing, and braving the temperatures as he made his way to the barn to get the first milking of the day done. Bellowing of the cows urged him quickly through his chores as he anticipated the comforting warmth of a hot breakfast prepared by Marie, followed by a relaxed day inside soaking up all possible warmth until it was time for evening chores. Once the weather changed and the days warmed to a much more reasonable 15 to 20 degrees, outdoor work could be resumed again. Then it was back to splitting wood, shelling corn or butchering a hog.

Lester and Marie had fine-tuned their butchering process to an art. From the time the carcass was hung in the tree by the garage, until the final foot of casing had been stuffed to become sausage, the process was orchestrated to flow from one step to the next, and, oh, how wonderful, the taste of fresh side pork or smelling a pork roast roasting slowly to golden perfection.

Once in a while a letter from his brother John brought Bill a smile as he read of John's activities. A large lake bordered the farm where

John was working and John wrote of ice fishing adventures. Some days the catch was good, others the result was several hours of being colder than he wanted to be and then returning home fishless.

John's letters in March talked about slush, rain, mud and then slush, rain, and mud again. By April things had warmed up and spring was in the air. Along with spring flowers poking up, John found a new activity to fill the time when all his chores were complete. A neighbor offered to pay him fifteen cents apiece for each pocket gopher he captured, then another neighbor upped the ante by offering twenty cents. John eagerly checked his traps each morning to see what the day's fortune might be!

In May of that year, Bill was pleased to be able to join his family as they celebrated Lorraine's 5th birthday. It didn't seem possible that she could be five so quickly. Bill managed a trip to town with Lester several weeks before and purchased pretty blue hair ribbons to give to his little sister as her birthday gift. Lester dropped him off on a Saturday night in mid May and Bill raced up the drive and opened the kitchen door as Karin was pulling a cake pan from the oven

"Oh, Bill. I am so pleased to see you again," Karin said. "You don't come home often enough."

"Hi, Mom," Bill responded. "I guess I don't want to wear out my welcome."

"Oh, you are such a tease," Karin responded quickly setting the hot cake on a waiting rack to cool and crossing the room to collect a long delayed mother-son hug.

As soon as Lorraine heard his voice, she bounded into the kitchen to collect her hug also. Soon the family gathered to enjoy supper together, and all enjoyed the birthday cake. Everyone wanted to talk at once telling of what had been going on with him or her and inquiring how the other was. Much too soon it was Sunday evening, and once again Bill prepared himself for the trip back to the Odegards'.

It was on this May visit that Lars shared with his son his good news of finding work through the WPA. His job with the canning factory at the "brick barn" had ended late last year and since then he had been unable to find regular work.

Shortly after his election in 1932, President Franklin Roosevelt had introduced his "New Deal", part of which included several programs to implement relief and recovery methods for workers so they could provide for their families. One program, the Public Works Administration, provided employment by sponsoring various kinds of building projects such as new roads, wayside rests, picnic areas with stone tables and benches and public swimming pools. Lars was pleased to be hired on to work at a park project going on in Mankato, about twenty miles from where the family was living.

In late September that year, Bill found himself once again in the dental chair as an aching molar could be treated only by extraction. This painful extraction and other fillings to preserve remaining teeth were matched only by painful payment for such procedures! While the two to three dollars per procedure may not seem like much; in 1935 it was a big chunk of Bill's monthly wages.

September turned to October, and October hurried past to November. Bill was able to come home to enjoy Thanksgiving with his family. Lester and Marie were planning to join their son Harold and his family at their nearby farm to celebrate the day. Uncle Carl and Aunt Gerda Johnson and two of their sons joined the Perssons for dinner that year. Karin had roasted two ducks for dinner and all who gathered, stuffed themselves into lumpy satisfaction. The conversation came around to remembering their first Thanksgiving in America and laughing again over their mistaken belief that Aunt Gerda had prepared Thanksgiving dinner in their honor when they first arrived.

"I never had such a wonderful meal before that day in my entire life," Karin said. "And to think it had been made just for us," she went on. Gerda and Carl smiled together in quiet amusement remembering that day also.

"And you, Bill," Lars began, "You just laid there on the blanket watching your cousins."

Bill nodded his head in assent and said, "Well, with Karl and Anna loading up on the potatoes, what else could I do?"

About four in the afternoon of that Thanksgiving day, Lars and Bill prepared for the trip back to the Odegard farm. Gerda, Carl and their children had already started out the drive on their way home again. All goodbyes said, each vehicle headed off in their own direction. About half an hour later as Lars and Bill neared the Odegard place; they could see several cars in the farmyard.

"I wonder what's going on," Bill began. "It's not like Lester to have such a crowd here this late in the day. Les and the missus were going to Harold's place for dinner. Whose cars are those?"

As they pulled into the yard, Bill identified the cars as belonging to Harold and another son, Evan. The county sheriff's car was there also. Bill and Lars got out of their car and walked to the kitchen door. Harold opened the door before they had the chance to knock.

"I seen you comin'," Harold said as they entered. "Bad news here, I'm afraid." He continued on, "Ma and Pa been killed. He run the car clean offa the road and down into the crick."

Evan stood up from where he had been sitting at the table with the sheriff and crossed the room to Lars and Bill. He extended his hand in silent welcome.

Lars took Evan's hand and hoped that some sensible, comforting words might find their way from his shock at the news. "I am so sorry to hear this," Lars stated. Bill was unable to say anything. He was inwardly reeling from the news and all he could manage was a handshake and a nod of his head.

Soon the sheriff had completed writing his report and left. Evan took control of the situation by announcing that he would stay the night if Bill would agree to help with evening chores that night and take care of the morning chores as well. Harold would go home to tend to his own stock. Lars announced that he had to get to work in Mankato the next day so he wouldn't be able to come back to pick Bill up again. "Don't worry about that," Evan said. "I'll see he gets home sometime tomorrow." The plans in place, Lars and Harold drove off in their respective cars. Evan and Bill wound up the night chores quickly and were back in the house again by 6:00.

"Reckon we don't need much supper," Evan announced. "Guess you ate as good as I did today."

That said, cheese sandwiches and canned pears became their meal and the evening passed without much conversation. Bill sat on the sofa in the quiet living room, thumbing through an old issue of Farm Journal. He remembered how he and Lester would enjoy their evenings together, sharing their amusement over the latest adventures of "Amos and Andy" on the radio.

The next morning Evan left Bill alone after they completed the morning milking. He was in a hurry to meet Harold so they could arrange their parent's funerals. Left to himself, Bill began packing up his things in his room. He filled a small cardboard box with his items, then placed them along with his suitcase by the kitchen door. The day passed slowly as Bill kept himself busy pounding a few nails in the board fence and playing several games of "fetch the stick" with the bewildered farm dog that spent most of her day vainly searching for Lester. Bill was not comfortable in the farmhouse by himself. He went in and out of the house several times to see to the wood stove, but he felt like an intruder without the Odegards there.

Evan returned about 4:30, they finished evening chores, then Bill was driven back home to the Perssons once again.

As he was getting out of the car, Evan announced to Bill that the funerals would be the next day, Saturday at 2:00 at the Methodist Church in Cleveland. That said, Evan bid Bill good evening and drove away. As Bill stood watching Evan drive away, his thoughts turned to Lester and what a good employer the Odegards had been. Where and how could he find another job when so many people were out of work?

CHAPTER 6:

MOVING ON

Just days after the Odegards' accident, life changed once again for Bill. At the Odegard funeral, a cousin of Lester's, Cy Gunders, learned that Bill needed a job. He stopped by the Persson home to see if Bill might come to work for him. Bill agreed and the following Sunday morning, Cy returned, this time to pick up Bill.

The Gunders farm was about five miles west of Le Sueur, and measured roughly eighty acres. About a third of the land was wooded and hilly, fit only for squirrels that shared domain with miscellaneous coon, a few woodchucks, and uncountable deer. Several beaver established residence in the small creek running through the bottom woods. There was just one old cow on the place. "Bossie gives just enough milk for me and the cats," Cy laughed.

Hogs were the mainstay of this farm and the usual count ran about sixty head; sixty noisy, squealing, rooting, smelly hogs. About thirty- five laying hens lived in the sagging, old chicken house and shared the run of the barnyard with one lazy, unidentifiable breed of hound dog, and innumerable cats.

The nearly fifty acres of tillable land was used to raise grains. Most acres were put into corn to provide feed for the herd of hogs, but Cy put in wheat whenever he got a hunch that this might be the year the market would be up.

Cy had never married and lived on his place alone. As soon as Bill stepped into the house, he got an idea of why this was so. The kitchen sink and table were piled high with dishes from days ago. The floor hadn't been cleaned in who knew how long. Bill noticed that the rest of the house was more of the same as he was led down the hall to a bedroom.

"This is where you can stay," Cy stated. Bill stepped into a room with a rumpled bed, an ancient relative's picture hanging askew, a dresser piled high with old newspapers and a pair of manure caked boots standing in one corner.

Having deposited Bill in the room, Cy strolled back into the kitchen calling out as he went, "I'll just go reheat some stew for us. Come eat when you get your stuff where you want it."

Bill glanced about the messy room wondering if he should put his shirts and underwear in the dresser or leave them in the suitcase. He pulled open a drawer, found it reasonably clean and placed his clothing in the dresser. He piled all the newspaper on the floor near the door and set out his bank, cigar box, toothbrush and comb. He decided not to straighten the bed as yet. There would be plenty of time to see to that later.

After the noontime meal of reheated stew, Cy walked back down the hall to his room and slammed the door shut. Bill figured that he must have been going to take a Sunday nap. "So what am I going to do with my time," Bill wondered to himself. He rummaged around the kitchen, found a metal dishpan, filled it with water and placed it on the kerosene stove to heat. When the water was hot, he found a bar of homemade soap on the sink and proceeded to tackle the mountain of dishes on the sink board and kitchen table. It was almost an hour later when the last dish was dried, pots put away and the table cleared and wiped clean.

After finishing in the kitchen, Bill wandered into the front room of the house. Here he found more piles of newspapers and stacks and stacks of magazines. "This man must save most every readable item that comes into the house," Bill thought to himself as he cleared a spot on the threadbare sofa and began looking through a magazine. He had just enjoyed thumbing through a National Geographic magazine and was reading about civilization in the South Pacific Islands, when Cy strolled into the room.

"Well, are you getting an education there, young fella?" Cy asked.

"Yes, sir," Bill responded. "Someday I'd like to see this part of the world for myself," he continued. "It would sure be great to get a first-hand look at those beaches and palm trees."

"Well, before you get that far, let me show you around the hog lot," Cy retorted. Then laughing at his joke, he went out the back door pausing long enough to grab his tattered old coat that hung by the back door.

Bill got up, found his own coat and joined his new boss as he entered the hog barn to begin the evening feeding chores.

From the first day he set foot in the hog barn, Bill knew that he didn't like the job of taking care of the pigs, and probably never would. After hog chores, he was shown what needed to be done with the chickens. First gather the eggs, and then make sure the "ladies", as Cy called them, had fresh food and water. Bill thought back to his previous two jobs that involved milking and feeding dairy cattle and decided on the spot that as soon as possible, he'd look around and see if a dairy farmer needed help. He did not like pigs, and chickens were a close second on the dislike list. He wrote home later to state "the best chicken he ever saw was the one on the Sunday dinner table!"

Bill's letters home continued sporadically, and he also managed to continue his correspondence with the Swanson's. He looked forward to a return letter now and then from Helen telling about her family and what they were doing. John, too, continued writing to Bill. His last letter told about having a crush on his employer's daughter. They had gone to a movie together, a Shirley Temple picture called the Littlest Rebel. He had also written about how the "boss" was able to sell pups for $10 each. The latest litter of eight was "sure a lot of dough for dogs!"

After a few weeks of living at Gunders place, Bill managed to get his room cleaned to his satisfaction. The walls and floor that hadn't seen soap and water in years were scrubbed to acceptable cleanliness. Once the bedroom was tolerable, Bill found himself on permanent cleaning duty around the house. Cy didn't seem bothered by a messy kitchen or clutter throughout the house and scarcely noticed Bill's efforts to make the place presentable. Bill figured if he was going to be living in this house, he was going to keep it as clean as he could.

Every Saturday, Cy loaded up all the eggs gathered that week and together he and Bill went into town to sell them. Usually the trip included a stop on Main Street where Cy joined his friends at the corner tavern to enjoy a beer or two. During this time, Bill usually wandered into the hardware store to admire the bicycles, and sometimes a stop at the dry goods store would be in order. His next letter to John mentioned that he had "squandered $1.50 on a pair of overalls." He also continued to send a dollar home almost every week to help his family as best he could.

Soon the daily chores became routine. January passed into February, and February into March. Bill was able to spend his 17th birthday at home with his family. The Sunday nearest his birthday was a real family reunion with Karl, Anna and John all at home for the day. Bill was delighted to enjoy the company of all his family once again, and how good it was to sit down to a good home cooked meal prepared by his mother that included meat, potatoes and vegetables, each item prepared and served separately, not in the usual "stew" he ate at Cy's place.

Cy's cooking skills, if one dared call them skills, were simple at best. Monday's roast "whatever", became stew the rest of the week, thrown together with potatoes and leftover gravy. Once in a while a can of corn or beans would be added to the meal for variety. Eggs were eaten often also, usually fried to hardened circles in a skillet next to slices of side pork. After a while the food all seemed the same to Bill, monotonous but sustainable.

The depression days were still upon everyone and it didn't seem that the economy would ever pick up again. From day to day, year-to-year, the struggle continued. Those without work continued to seek a job, while those with a job were squeezing every cent of their meager payments to cover the care of themselves or their families. Through the passing weeks of hated pig chores, Bill endured, grateful because he was one of the lucky ones. He had a job, distasteful as it was, a roof over his head, and plenty to eat, mundane as that was.

1936 continued on. The crops were planted, and early June's hint of hot weather became the real thing by mid month. The weekly trips to town with Cy on Saturday mornings often resulted in Bill meeting his friend Fred Schmidt. Once in a while the two young men planned to meet again Saturday night and see what they could find to do. Weekly band concerts were held during the summer months at Stewart Park. At one such concert, they met two young girls, Margie and Evelyn, and the girls agreed to sit with them to listen to the music. After seeing the girls home, Fred would drive Bill back to Cy's farm.

Bill so wished that he could afford to get a vehicle of his own so he wouldn't be dependent on Cy or Fred to provide transportation. Earlier in May, Bill noticed a tarp- draped form sitting in one corner of the machine shed. Boards, buckets, and miscellaneous tools came to rest on top of the tarp, the pile growing precariously as Cy passed by and set an item down.

One evening as they sat together on the front porch, trying to escape the oppressive heat in the house, Bill asked, "Cy, what is that you have stored in the machine shed under the tarp?"

"Oh, that's an old car that my dad owned. He bought it new in 1920 and hardly drove it enough to break in the engine," Cy responded. "Come on. Let's go take a look at 'er." Quickly he left the porch and walked across the yard to the shed, with Bill just a step behind. Together he and Bill cleared the accumulated items stacked on top of the tarp, then raising the tarp, gazed at a black 1920 Ford.

"The Old Man just never got the hang of driving a car," Cy offered. "When I started driving, we bought my truck to haul the farm stuff, and I took him around where he needed to go. One day he covered the car with this tarp and there she's set all these years. Probably won't run anymore."

"Spose I could try to get it running?" Bill asked. "Help yourself," Cy answered, and then turned away and headed back to the house to retire for the night.

Bill stood for a few minutes gazing at the old car. He didn't know where to start and even if he did, he wasn't sure he would be able to get it running. All he had to draw on was the experience of watching Lars work on the Persson family car. The combination of youth and hopeful optimism would surely help him figure things out and get this old "Lizzie" running again he thought as he poked under the hood, tightening a spark plug here and tugging on the fan belt there.

For the next few weeks after he had completed the evening hog and chicken chores, Bill gulped down whatever was for supper, and then hurried out to the machine shed to snatch a few minutes of remaining daylight to work on the old car. He cleaned the carburetor, replaced the spark plugs, and made sure that the radiator hose and fan belt were still functional. Deflated inner tubes were patched and pumped to new life. Finally he felt ready to see if "Lizzie" would run.

Cy had watched this activity from the comfort of his front porch rocker. "Let's give 'er a try," he called out to Bill. Together they pushed the car out into the yard and Cy stepped to the front of the vehicle to give it a crank. "Get up in the seat and we'll see if she goes," he said to Bill. Quickly Bill hopped into the car and after five or six cranks, the engine roared to life. "Give 'er the gas," Cy shouted above the noise. Bill did, and slowly and noisily the old Ford moved around the farmyard.

"Hiyuh," Cy shouted gleefully as Bill drove the car around the yard and back to the shed. "You did it, Billy Boy. You got 'er goin'," Cy said. Bill was so pleased that his efforts of the past several weeks had paid off, and the old car showed it still had some life left in it. If only he could afford to buy the car for his own.

"Well, now you got 'er running, you better buy 'er for your own," Cy remarked. "You can have 'er for say, twenty-five dollars. You can pay me so much a month."

Bill could not believe what he was hearing. It would have been reward enough to know that his mechanical skills had coaxed life back into the ancient engine but now this offer to sell him the car, well, this was really beyond anything he could hope for. For a little while the extra dollars sent home would go towards his car and daily doses of unpleasant hog and chicken chores somehow just didn't seem so bad anymore.

Bill decided that he couldn't go on referring to the car as "Lizzie." Now that it was his, she needed a better name. "I'll call her "Mary Ellen," Bill remarked to himself, the name just popping into his head from nowhere. "Won't Fred laugh when I tell him about my new girlfriend," Bill smiled.

Fred did enjoy a good laugh over Bill's new "girlfriend." "I can't believe that Cy would sell this old 'beaut' to you," he remarked to Bill. "Well, he did and I took him up on the offer," Bill replied. "But it was up to me to get Mary Ellen up and running again," he went on. "Bet you didn't know that I was such a great mechanic," he added. Fred just grinned and nodded his head.

The Saturday night "socials" became ritual for the two young men. They usually arranged to meet at Jones Café and see if any young ladies there might care to accompany them on the evening's activities. Once the band concerts ended for the summer, they either went to the movies, a barn dance at Schwartz's or just spent a couple hours in animated conversation as they shared news of their previous week's happenings. Fred confided to Bill that he really thought that Evelyn was a swell girl and he preferred to be with her instead of anyone else. They soon became a couple and talk turned to their future plans together.

Bill enjoyed the company of all their girl acquaintances. It didn't matter to him if Margie, Bernice or Katie was a part of the Saturday foursome. He enjoyed the company of each without preference to any one in particular.

Margie did appear to be the most forward of the girls. It seemed that she could never get close enough to him, hold hands long enough and when they shared a first kiss, she tried to claim his company exclusively. Margie had said that she was fifteen, but when Bill learned that she was only thirteen that summer, he backed off quickly. Getting all wrapped up in someone so young could be nothing but trouble he decided, and he didn't care for somebody who didn't tell the truth. He chose to be with other girls, who were closer in age and interests. Bill was more than relieved when Margie's family moved away in August and he no longer had to avoid her flirtations or think of excuses to offer when he had spent Saturday night with Grace, Irene or Ruth.

Margie aside, it had been a glorious seventeenth summer for Bill with wonderful memories of good times shared between friends. However, even though there were lots of good times to be had and so much pride and enjoyment in owning "Mary Ellen", Bill felt a kind of restlessness. Was slopping hogs and tending chickens all there would be to his life? He really couldn't see himself continuing along as he was; working for Cy all week long and still not really getting ahead, then blowing an extra dollar every weekend with his friends with nothing but an empty pocket on Monday morning. There had to be an alternative.

Fred's older brother had joined the Civilian Conservation Corps and wrote home telling of his adventures hundreds of miles away. "The "grub" was good and a fella could make $30 a month, plus get an issue of clothing", Donald had written. One was required to send home twenty-five dollars every month but Bill thought, why not. I'll get fed and get some new clothes and maybe I'll get shipped to some- place I've never been. It would be good to be able to help more with expenses at home too. He'd have "Mary Ellen" all paid off at once and could even have Karin put a few dollars away in his savings account. Who knew how much he would have in the account when he got home again. Joining up seemed an appealing undertaking.

The Civilian Conservation Corps, like the WPA, was a program of President Franklin Roosevelt's New Deal. It was originally started to provide employment for sons of those men in America who were on relief. Soon it was expanded to all able- bodied young men aged seventeen to twenty-five. In addition to providing employment in Depression Days, CCC promoted environmental conservation. Some of the crews worked on building roads, others helped build new park facilities, and some spent time learning how to fight forest fires.

All of this physically hard work, overshadowed the monotony of daily routine on the Gunders farm. Bill was sure the CCC would be a better deal than being a "housekeeper", and a hog and chicken man!

All of August and September Bill mulled over his choices; continue on at Cy's place or strike off on a new adventure. Finally he made up his mind and began the process involved in joining the CCC. As soon as he was certain everything was in order, he braced himself to tell Cy of his decision.

Surprisingly, Cy was not upset to learn of Bill's unrest. He reminded Bill that he too, had been a young man once and longed for some adventure beyond the confines of his farm life in Minne- sota. Bill finished out the month of September with Cy, and then went home to spend a few days with his family before going off to the unknown.

Lars was most supportive of his son's decision to join the CCC, but Karin was not at all sure she could bear to have a son leaving for some long distant location. But Bill had made up his mind, the papers had been signed and now there was no turning back.

On the morning of Thursday October 9, 1936, Bill and Lars got into "Mary Ellen" for the drive to Mankato to the CCC office. The conversation between the two was mostly small talk about how the corn would soon be ready to pick and "wasn't the sky a beautiful blue today."

The twenty-five miles to Mankato went by quickly; it was surprising how quickly the buildings of the town came into view. Bill suggested that they stop for a cup of coffee before proceeding to the armory. Once the coffee stop was completed, it was time to continue on to the CCC office. Getting out of the car, Lars assured Bill that he would see to it that "Mary Ellen" was put up on blocks until Bill returned home again. The last goodbyes between father and son started with a handshake, but soon became a loving embrace. Lars watched as Bill stepped into the building, pausing long enough for one final wave before leaving.

CHAPTER 7:

LEAVING MINNESOTA

Bill looked around the large open room to see if any of the almost eighty men might be someone that he knew. The only person that he recognized was Johnny Gries, who lived on a large dairy farm near Elysian. The boys had met several times at Hardegger's dance hall when they attended Saturday night dances. Johnny's cousin Katie was a friend of Bill's from Le Sueur. As soon as Johnny saw Bill, he walked across the room to where Bill stood, extending a welcoming hand.

"Hello, Bill," Johnny began. "Looks like we're both looking for some changes, huh?" he questioned. "What a surprise to see you here," Bill responded. "Where do you think we'll be headed?" he added.

But there was little time for more conversation as the army officer, clipboard in hand, bellowed out orders to the wide-eyed enrollees.

"Line up there by the wall and count off by threes," he blustered. Quickly the recruits did as they were ordered.

"All right, now," the orders continued. "All 'ones' and 'twos' proceed out the door to the rear and load up in the buses there."

Bill had counted off as a three and he and the remaining "threes" continued standing by the wall as the other groups filed out. Johnny shouted a quick "good luck" to Bill as his group filed out the door.

After the last group was gone, the officer passed out meal tickets to those still in the room. "Here's a meal ticket for your grub," he bellowed. "There's a restaurant in the next block by the train station. Be at the station and ready to board the train at 4:00PM. Don't be late. We ain't easy on stragglers."

The train left the Mankato depot promptly at 4:10PM, and as ordered, there were no stragglers! At 7:00 PM the train pulled into Minneapolis and all boarded a streetcar for the last leg of their journey to Fort Snelling. As they stepped from the streetcar, the small-town and country boys were all eyes as they looked around the fort. Bill remembered history lessons that explained the importance the fort had played in the early settlement of Minnesota, and now here he was seeing those same old buildings and standing on the brink of history himself!

The rest of the evening was spent listening to short lectures about just what to expect of CCC life. By 9:30 most were more than grateful to plop down on their assigned cots. Some conversations continued for a while, but most were sleeping almost as soon as their heads were on their pillows. It had been a tiring, eventful day for everyone.

Early Friday morning the enrollees were ushered into a huge armory type building and told to stand in line to fill out more necessary paperwork for their enlistment. The CCC was under the jurisdiction of the United States Army and the military regimentation was evident. After completing the paperwork, they stood in another line for their first issue of equipment. They were given a mess tin, cup, knife, fork and spoon, bed- clothes, water canteen and a luggage sack. Then they were moved to still more lines for a series of different shots. Most passed through the shot lines without incident, but one fellow fainted just as he found himself next to face the needle. Quickly Bill helped the recruit to his feet and brushed aside any discomfort the embarrassed young man might have felt by assuring him that he wasn't the only one feeling "woozy."

'Hey Buddy, I was almost down there with you," Bill stated. "Maybe next time you'll be picking me up," he joked.

By late afternoon all the entrance preparations and disbursements were complete. The Mankato contingent was joined with several other groups from different areas of the state. Together the new recruits were fed a light supper, and even more exhausted then they were the previous evening, the men gratefully fell into their cots well before ten o'clock. With much tossing and turning they struggled to find a comfortable position, cushioning limbs as best they could from the discomfort from the shots they had been given earlier in the day.

Saturday morning all were wakened early to stand formation before "mess" at 7:00AM. Further physical exams were completed. Nobody wanted another day of standing in "shot lines" and most did avoid further inoculations. Issued gear was checked, and then rechecked. By now all were familiar with the "Army" way of doing things!

By early evening, encumbered with newly issued gear, plus what they had brought with them from home, they were loaded on army busses that would transport them to the train depot in St. Paul. Upon arrival at the train station, the CCC officer in charge herded them to their departure gate. Bill guessed there must have been at least fifty young men getting on the westbound train that evening. Not all had the same final destination, but all were excited about the trip and wondered what CCC life had in store for them.

The recruits were all assigned sleeper cars for the trip. Most would be on the train for several days and this concession to passenger comfort would be remembered with appreciation later when comfort was exchanged for utility as they got used to sleeping on army cots! It had been another long day for all and they were glad when the porter made up the sleeper beds. They settled in without objection and soon most were asleep, lulled by the rhythmic sound and sway of the train as it traveled into the night.

On the day of his arrival in Cathlamet, Washington, Bill wrote what would become a regular exchange of letters home to his family, all the while looking forward to their responses back to him. His first letter began:

****

Cathlamet, Wash.
October 13, 1936
Dear Folks,
Arrived here about 8 o'clock this morning. I certainly was glad to get here after that long trip. We left St. Paul Saturday night. Rode on sleeping cars all the way. Woke up way out in South Dakota. Went through part of N.D. too. The Dakota's are even worse than I thought they were. The trees are scarcer than fleas on a goldfish. It's hilly, rocky and dry. It seemed miles between each straggling village. The farm places were ten times as far apart as in Minnesota.

Everything seemed dry and disappointed. Even the jackrabbits looked disgusted. We set our time back 1 hr. in Dakota by the Missouri River. We were about half way or more across Montana before Sunday night.

Montana looked almost as dry and desolate. Here and there we could see the carcass or skeleton of some dead animal. We saw a few hundred sheep, but no large herds of cattle. In the central part of the state, they raised quite a few sugar beets. Some irrigation ditches could be seen.

Sunday night they put an electric engine on the train. Monday morning when we woke up we were deep in the Rockies, but still in Montana. Went through Idaho on Monday, mountains all the way.

The Rockies certainly are beautiful. Winding rivers, deep canyons and green pine trees. We went through a lot of tunnels there in the hills. Most of the way we could see pine stumps ten and twenty feet high, scorched black by forest fires. All are standing there as grim monuments of somebody's carelessness.

We only got out for exercise twice on the whole trip, once in N.D. and once in Idaho. Went through part of Washington, the city of Spokane before night. We were at Kelso this morning (Tuesday). Were hauled out here to camp 26 miles by truck.

The grub on the train wasn't so bad if we would have gotten about 3 times as much. Two slices of bakers bread, no more, along with some potatoes, plus and apple and rotten coffee. No sugar. Set time back another hour in Idaho.

The camp here is situated about 100 miles from Seattle, on the Columbia River. Oregon is right across the river. I think the coast is about 75 miles away. This seems to be a well- equipped camp with a lot of good buildings. The town is about a mile away, mountains all around. We got a swell feed for dinner. Bread, beans, coffee, relish, butter, one piece of meat, and believe it or not, sugar.

Before we left Fort Snelling we got a shot in the arm. Had a stiff arm for a couple days. I guess we get a couple shots here too.

We got an issue of clothes. There's 3 sets of underwear, an overseas cap, two army shirts, two pair of overalls, a pair of shoes, 4 pairs of socks, two towels, a jacket, 2 large coats, a canvass belt, and a necktie. We also got thread and needles, soap and case, toothbrush, toothpaste, razor, shaving cream, thimble, toothbrush case, shaving brush and comb.

There's a two- cent tax on every dollar's worth of merchandise you buy here.

Please excuse my scribbles. I'm sitting on my cot using my suitcase for a table. They say there are about 150 men in this camp now. The company number is 4766, all from Minn.

There were about 18 cars on our train. Half of them were switched at Spokane and sent to Oregon CCCs.

I met Carl Ullberg at Fort Snelling. He signed for the CCC's too. I don't know where he was sent.

The 3 Larson boys are here at camp, one Bulpaff from Lake Jefferson too.

Now that I've gone through the Dakotas and Montana, I really know how wonderful Minnesota is, even if we don't think so at times.

According to the old timers it rains here every day almost or else there is fog.

I'm quite a ways from home now, more than 2000 miles. I never thought I could get tired of riding a train but I sure changed my mind in a hurry.

We have electric lights here at camp. There's a canteen where you can get cigarettes and candy.

It's raining heavy right now. I imagine it takes about 4 or 5 days for a letter to get home.

I'll write more soon. In the meantime, love to all, Bill

****

The first full day of CCC camp in Cathlamet, Washington was spent getting gear squared away in the barracks. Bill was assigned the bunk next to the young man who had fainted after getting his shots at Fort Snelling. Norbert Stumpf was from a town not far from the Le Sueur area. Soon the two found themselves becoming good friends. After learning that Norbert's friends back home called him "Weasel", all the fellow CCC members called him by that name too.

The main camp consisted of stark look-alike buildings. Three served as barracks, one as a mess hall and another served as a canteen. Part of the canteen building was designated as living quarters for the officer in charge of the camp. Three other subordinates shared an additional, partitioned room in the same building. The last building in the compound was used to store tools and supplies.

All of the buildings were sparse, lean and simple. The exterior walls were tar-papered in an attempt to keep out cold weather. The interior walls were unfinished. Whitewash had been applied to make them look clean. The open beamed ceilings held in the hot air in the summer and allowed cold air in during the winter. The roofs were simply a double layer of tarpaper. In each of the buildings a wood-burning stove belched out smoke and just enough heat to keep items or human inhabitants from freezing.

Calls to mess and morning wake up were announced by the ringing of a large school bell situated on the mess hall roof. There was also an information area where world news and announcements of camp interest were posted behind a glass frame for all to see. The men regularly checked the camp announcements to see where their work assignments for the week would be.

One main cement sidewalk ran between the mess hall and the canteen. Log lined pathways of gravel connected the barracks to the main sidewalk and a wooden rail fence ran along the outside perimeter of camp #4766.

Each "rookie" took his turn being initiated to camp life. It was up to the discretion of the "regulars" to decide what kind of humiliation would be dealt and to whom. Most times it was simply just a week of making up a "regular's" cot or serving his mess duty; "sentenced to slavery" as it was called. Some "rookies" were forced to wear a paper sign hung from their neck with their "inmate number" on it. All this activity was in good fun and nobody ever felt the treatment to be more than simple indoctrination of a newcomer. All at the camp, including the "regulars", had been through initiation. The camp supervisor considered the ritual something that strengthened the bonds of friendship between the young men. Most of them had never been so far away from home and the good-natured joking helped to prevent terrible pangs of being homesick from becoming overwhelming.

Soon Bill fell into the daily routine of camp which was: "Up at six-thirty, make fire, sweep the barracks, wash up. Roll call and 'Pledge of Allegiance' in front of the mess hall. Breakfast at 7:00. Go to work at 7:30. Back for dinner at 11:30 and on the job again at 12:45. Through with work at 3:30."

Saturdays were clean up days. The men did their laundry by hand, rubbing vigorously on washboards to remove a week's worth of sweat, mud and food remnants. After personal chores, they might have a game of horseshoe or go for a hike in the mountains. Sometimes they ventured as far as Kelso, twenty-six miles away and thumbed a ride back to camp again.

Periodically some of the men were taken from the main camp to "side camp", the site of a particular work project usually ten to twenty miles from the main campsite. Conditions at "side camp" were a lot more primitive with no electricity, which meant no radios for entertainment. Gas lamps were used for light, which hardly mattered since no magazines or newspapers were available to read anyhow. Bill observed that it was easy to become "brush-batty" without radios or reading material. Some evenings were spent playing poker for matches. On occasion the men were loaded into the open end of the work truck and hauled into town to see a movie. The admission was twenty cents!

Bill's letter of October 24, 1936 said that his group was returned to the main camp for another shot in the arm. The shots were canceled and instead twenty-five men were sent to Vancouver for firefighting duty. This was a long two hundred mile trip in the back of a truck. Bill counted himself lucky not to have made this trip.

The rest of the group who remained after the firefighters left, returned to side camp and continued their road-building job in the forest. Once in a while they encountered wild life. The side camp talk was pretty animated the day a bear was spotted. Another time two hunters passed through with their kill of the day, a large bob- cat. Bill decided to ask Karin to see about sending his rifle to him so that he might go hunting on his off time. Within a week or two, a package with the rifle, carefully wrapped in newspapers, arrived.

He also wrote to John asking him to buy a share of "Mary Ellen" as Bill stated he really could use some money for personal spending. Letters from Karin and a note once in a while from Jana sharing news from herself and Lorraine brightened mail call for Bill. Those times when he heard from loved ones at home made the days of being so far away more bearable.

When a letter arrived from Karin with two dollars in it, Bill wrote back that same evening thanking his mother. His savings account was growing much slower than he had planned but what could he do. He needed money to get along at camp too. The four or five dollars a month the men could keep from their pay for personal spending just didn't go very far when each had to buy all their personal supplies from it.

In mid-November, the men were hauled back to main camp for the delayed typhoid shot they were scheduled to have earlier. While there, Bill purchased a flashlight, bottle of ink, some envelopes and stamps. They were also allowed to bring some books to side camp from the library at the main camp.

The workers were given four days off for Thanksgiving and they were able to return to the main camp for their stay. While there, Bill telegrammed his parents on Thanksgiving day:

> *10:15 AM 11-26-36*
> *To Dad and Mother with all my heart I wish*
> *I were with you at home today. My thankful*
> *love to you always*
> *Bill*

The next day he was sent on fire-fighting detail about seventy miles from camp, riding there as all did, in the back of an army truck. The four-day vacation had dwindled to two. He wrote, "almost froze to death going out and then almost roasted at the fire." He also shared sad news about a buddy who died after having an appendicitis operation.

Once back at side camp, the work on road building continued. The men first crushed rock, then spread it making a roadway through the forest. The rains were pouring down and after wading in water to spread the rock and mucking around in the clay soil all day, they looked like "clay dummies." Bill decided that on the next trip to main camp he would try to purchase some rubber boots to keep his feet a little drier. They had been promised an issue of rubber boots but it didn't appear to be coming.

Bill found the food at side camp to be much better than what was served at the main camp. One Sunday evening he wrote to John telling him about what had to eat that day.

Breakfast: coffee, toast and butter, corn flakes, boiled eggs, 1 banana (everyone had a cigarette because somebody had a birthday)

Dinner: Baked potatoes, corn, macaroni, bread and butter, coffee, Jell-O, cookies, salad

Supper: Potato salad, beans, tomatoes, bread-butter, coffee, baloney, peach sauce, salad

Certain items were limited in number and Bill stated, "If you don't grab quick, you're out of luck. Sometimes the coffee tastes like tar, the eggs are raw or the bananas rotten. But little things like that don't bother us. We eat anything that is put in front of us."

The fact that January of 1937 was cold came as no surprise to anyone at CCC camp since December of 1936 had primed them to frigid conditions. Morning clean-up time took on an added challenge when the water pipes were frozen for two weeks and no running water was available to the men. Their choice for washing was either beating everyone else to the hot water heating on the stoves, or to quickly splash freezing water over their faces from the icy creek running by the camp side.

Working the jack-hammer at the road site and being able to set off dynamite charges made the days pass quickly. Bill wrote home that he had received a Christmas card from Karl and was still in shock over that!

It may have been the sameness of the cold days, boredom or real dissatisfaction with the food served that prompted the men at the main camp to go on a food strike. But bad as they might have thought the food was, the punishment for leading the strike was severe. Nine fellows were dismissed because of their role in the strike. The news of the strikers' punishment filtered back to side camp where the men were also frustrated with their rations.

During the first weeks and months of CCC living, the food served was actually all right, but in time what was once deemed "good" became "just all right" and then fell to just plain intolerable.

So the men at side camp also resorted to a food strike to express their displeasure. Their punishment was much less severe. Nobody was dismissed but they did have to work an extra half day for the time missed during the strike.

When snows in January stopped progress on the road construction, the work turned to cutting down dead trees. This process was done mostly as a means of fire protection. For the most part, the trees ranged from four inches in diameter to over four feet across. Most were about 100 feet high and made a thundering crash when they fell to the ground. The snows also made hiking on the off days interesting as animal tracks were more apparent. Several times Bill found himself following a set of wild-cat tracks through the forest, but he was never able to manage to see the cat itself and get off a shot.

The snows of January gave way to rains, and in a short time Bill bemoaned the fact that the promised rubber boot issue to the men still was not materializing. Nobody seemed to know what the delay was, so the wet shoes and grumbling continued.

Every weekend the men took their turns working kitchen duty. This amounted to some light food preparation, serving the food and cleaning up. It wasn't a job that Bill particularly looked forward to, but wasn't so bad since it came around on a rotational basis. On the other hand, KP duty afforded the kitchen workers opportunity to help themselves to everything and anything that could be eaten! Apples and oranges were particular favorites to "cop" on to.

Another amusement that Bill allowed himself was taking pictures of the area where he was. From his meager funds, he purchased a box camera for two dollars and a roll of film for fifty cents. He enjoyed taking multiple snapshots of the camp and also of new-found friends at camp. Even though photography put a considerable dent in his personal money allotment each week, it was a pastime that he genuinely enjoyed. The cost of the film and developing of the pictures somehow seemed worth it all when he could share the sights of Washington with his family. Bill was truly grateful for those times when pictures arrived in Washington from home too. He loved seeing how his kid sisters grew and changed as different pictures came to him.

In addition to the occasional letters from Karin, several of Bill's friends from Le Sueur continued corresponding with him. Katie and Vivian were especially faithful in writing to him. He commented to Karin that he hardly knew Vivian, but nonetheless it was always good to receive a letter during mail call. He even welcomed letters from that pesky Margie who lived in South Dakota with her family after leaving Le Sueur. She chattered on and on about school activities and going to dances on the weekends. While he was glad to get letters from anyone, the distance of miles between he and Margie was something that he didn't mind at all! That book had been closed long ago.

On a pleasant Sunday in early March of 1937, Bill and some of his friends from camp took a boat ride on the Columbia River going all the way to the Pacific Ocean. The scenery was beautiful and the young men were amazed at how quickly the seventy-mile river trip passed. The price was right too. They paid the grand sum of one dollar each! After reaching the beach area, they took off their shoes and socks and waded into the ocean. They frolicked and played in the water like children until it was time for the return trip back to camp again.

"Did you ever think you'd see this much water in your life "Weasel"? Bill called to his friend.

"I sure got a whole lot more respect for old Christopher Columbus now," answered Weasel. Bill's delight with his first view of the ocean was shared with Lars and Karin in a letter home a few days later when he wrote vivid descriptions of how the huge foamy waves were roaring when they rolled back on the water.

Once back to a regular workweek in camp, the rains that had started in January continued day after dreary day. All of the workers struggled to face the combination of constant bad weather and dissatisfaction with their food and living conditions; not to mention the ache of being separated from loved ones. When they just couldn't imagine one more week of misery, they made their choices and quit CCC to return home again. Being jobless at home seemed the better option for the moment.

When Bill had been in CCC for almost six months, he figured that he could hang on a while longer. He liked the hard physical work, the companionship was great and even the food must have agreed with him because he tipped the scales at 180 pounds. He wrote home requesting that Karin send some of his summer clothing since what he was wearing would soon be uncomfortable in the warmth of summer.

The requested clothing arrived in Washington in April and Bill wrote his thanks home commenting once again about their weather that never seemed to vary much between rain and mud! He also shared his elation on seeing sixty-four new campers, who arrived from Minnesota, taking the place of those who had left earlier.

Letters came off and on from those who had returned to their homes again. Bob Courtland wrote that "CCC just wasn't what it was cracked up to be," and Spike Ranning told of his "swell" new job that paid him the handsome sum of $18 per week". There were times when Bill pondered if he had made the right decision to stay in when so many had left earlier. But he was counting on getting all his additional pay by summer and that would be a tidy sum. On his next six- day leave, he was going to go to hitchhike to Seattle or Portland and see what that part of the country looked like.

After a letter arrived from Karl in April, Bill wrote back about what life was like in CCC Camp now that the miserable winter had turned into spring. His take on camp life as of that writing had improved somewhat. He described the location of the camp near Cathlamet. "We're building roads here for fire trails in the state forest. Most of the timber has been logged off though. One crew is building bridges, and there are lots of creeks here. The camp is in the foothills of the Cascade Range of mountains. On clear days we can see Mt. Hood in Oregon and St. Helens in Washington. They are about sixty miles from here. The weather stays the same. We have so much rain that I may be getting webbed feet soon."

The next letter that Bill wrote to Karl some weeks later, painted a much different picture. There were no words describing the location of camp or what beauty there was in the area. Instead he wrote about his concern that he would soon be on forest fire fighting duty and he did not like this at all. It was grueling work. First there was the uncomfortable ride in the bed of a truck to the fire site. The danger of flaming branches or trees falling was constant as the crews dug ditches or felled timber in order to create a fire line to contain the blazes. The heat of the fire and the constant roar of the flames over-head added to the total misery of the situation.

Bill desperately explained to Karl a plan to get released from CCC. He suggested that he needed to have a letter from an employer in Minnesota stating that a job was available for him there. He asked Karl to write a letter stating that Karl owned a farm and was ready to provide employment there for Bill. His next letter to Karin stated basically the same thing; he was tired of CCC life and wanted to get out!

By late May the forest fire season was going strong and Bill's chances of dismissal were dim. It was a very difficult time period for him because he found himself completely dreading the thought of one more day of the hated firefighting duty. He would have given anything to be at home again.

If something didn't turn up to release him soon, maybe he would to go to Seattle and take an examination to join the Navy!

In early June of 1937, Bill finally managed to quit his service with CCC and his frustrating situation came to an end. He boarded the North Coast Limited train in Seattle on June 15 and arrived back in St. Paul, Minnesota two and a half days later. Another train ride took him to Le Center, and from there he hitchhiked home to the welcoming warmth of his family. Jana and Lorraine just couldn't hug him hard and long enough to show their elation. Tears streamed down Karin's face when she couldn't find words to say to him. Lars kept repeating, "Bill, it is so good to have you home again."

After resting up for a few days and enjoying the euphoria of being home again, Bill applied for work at the Minnesota Valley Canning Company in Le Sueur. He was hired to work at Rush River Vinery where acres of peas were separated from the vines, placed in boxes and hauled to the canning factory site where they were processed into canned peas. His job behind a pitchfork lifting the pea-laden vines paid him well and by the end of pea pack he had cleared a grand total of $124.

Bill and one or both of his brothers spent lots of time together when they could that summer of 1937. They enjoyed swimming at Lake Washington, going to dances, or roller- skating. Bill and John took in an air-show in Mankato where they went for a plane ride in one of the small planes that was part of the air-show. They talked of that experience for weeks afterwards. John had taken over the payments on "Mary Ellen" shortly after Bill left for CCC camp and now they both enjoyed the sheer pleasure of just hopping into the car and riding up and down Main Street. One Saturday night while on a spin down the outskirts of St. Peter, John took a corner too fast and the car upset.

As the car lay on its side in the street with both brothers still inside, John called to Bill, "Are you OK, Bill?" "Yeah, just banged my elbow pretty good," came the answer.

In July when the pea pack was over and threshing season had started, Bill found work on a threshing crew. It was good to have funds and be able to take a girl to a show or roller-skating. Vivian, the girl who had been a faithful correspondent while he was away at CCC Camp, was a frequent date. When Vivian was busy, he just hooked up with Peggy or Irene. Bill wasn't ready to settle down with just one steady girl. It was just too much fun being with lots of different people.

In August that summer, Bill decided it was time for him to own a car again. The next trip to Mankato was specifically for that purpose. Bill purchased a 1928 Chevy sedan for the magnificent sum of $50.00. It was good to have his own transportation once more but car troubles and repairs became a constant in his life. It seemed that he'd replace the tires and then a rod would go out. A new radiator hose led to some other mechanical problem. He joked that this car was about as expensive as a wife!

Bill went back to working at the canning factory after threshing was over. The corn pack ended on September 3 and he decided he needed a trip out of town. He hopped a freight train in Le Sueur, got to Minneapolis, and then climbed into a different boxcar on a train going to Fargo. In Dickenson, North Dakota the local sheriff apprehended sixteen "Knights of the Road" including Bill. After a "free trip" of 600 miles, he had to shell out $9.50 to pay for a ticket back home again! One more adventure to laugh about and share with his brothers!

In October, Anna became engaged to the young man she had been dating for some time. Bill genuinely liked Mel and thought this would be a good match for his older sister. He shared their excitement about getting married and wished them well as they made plans for the future.

When the time came to pick field corn, Bill and John found jobs helping farmers in the Lakota, Iowa area. They got together on weekends so the work filled days in the fields went quickly as they anticipated being able to see each other on Sunday. Bill proudly wrote home telling about days of picking eighty to eighty-five bushels of corn. It was very hard work but still a relief from remembered days of crushing rock with a jackhammer or fighting forest fires!

Both brothers were home again with the family in mid December and celebrated a quiet Christmas there with everyone. Bill took note of Karin not feeling physically well after Christmas dinner but decided she must have eaten something that did not agree with her. He questioned her, "Are you all right, Mom?" Before he could think much more of it Karin responded. "It must have been the cranberry relish that didn't sit well." Nothing more was said.

Before the end of December, Bill once again was out looking for work. This time he heard of a job with Wettergren Dairy in St. Peter. He had no idea what this involved, but he needed work and was open to whatever came his way. Very quickly he learned about milking fifty head of cows twice a day and between milking times, doing all kinds of chores around the dairy. Feeding cows and mucking out the stalls was hardly a position of choice, but thinking back on the pig experience at Cy Gunder's place made it easier. He remembered his words at that time about never wanting to work with pigs again. He'd take working with the cows for now. They didn't smell quite as bad as pigs, and he was earning room and board plus $34.00 a month. Hundreds of others would have jumped at the chance to work at the dairy. So many were still struggling through the depressed American economy. Again, Bill counted himself lucky to have employment of any kind.

Anna and Mel were married in March. Bill was so pleased when Mel asked him to be his best man. Mel's sister was the maid of honor and everyone enjoyed themselves at the small church reception afterwards. The young couple happily started their married life with only the barest essentials and a ton of hope that things would get better through the years.

By the time of the wedding, it was obvious that Karin's Christmas time illness was a lot more than cranberry relish. She looked so drained and the heaviness of pregnancy was about her. Bill's visits home grew farther and farther apart. It was so hard to see his mother looking so miserable and staying away prevented him from observing her uncomfortable changes from week to week.

The new baby was born on June 11, 1938, a little girl who was named Katrina Corrine. Karin was physically and emotionally drained after the baby came and found caring for her family nearly impossible. Jana at age eleven did all she could to help with the baby and Lorraine but she was just a child herself and things never seemed to get caught up. As time went by, neglect on all sides became evident. Although Lars stepped up to help as much as he could when he came home from work, he worried more and more as the days went by that Karin would not be able to get through the "sadness" after the birth of this latest baby. There was discouragement throughout the Persson household.

All over the world discouragement was evident as news spread about the German annexation of Austria. Hitler's plan to rule Europe began subtly and soon led to persecution of anyone standing in his way. Many ethnic peoples felt his power as they lost their property and then their very lives as this madman set into place his method of operation along the way to his plan for world domination. The enormity of the advances were not immediately evident but the long tentacles of Nazism had begun their treacherous outreach.

Nor did the western world have a total grasp of the scope and size of Japan's plans to rule the world. China was already suffering under the Japanese invasion of 1937. These insidious advances involved the killing of helpless, innocent people. Seizing of their lands went on without objection as unaffected populations continued living daily lives in peaceful oblivion; their eyes and ears closed to what was happening in the rest of the world.

Many countries, including the United States, appeared to be unconcerned, even uncaring about what was happening. If the atrocities were not taking place in their respective backyards, and they were not personally affected, it didn't seem that it was their concern. Furthermore, what could they do about the situation, short of taking up arms themselves. For some, the memories of bloody involvement in WWI remained vivid and no one was anxious to take to battle again.

Adding to the situation was the fact that the Americans still were fighting different personal battles at home. Their worries did not extend to the far corners of the world. Their immediate concern was providing food and shelter for their families in the ongoing Depression Years. They preferred to remain living in peaceful neutrality and let the rest of the warring nations settle their own problems.

As the days and months went by and the invasions and brutality continued, it became evident that peaceful neutrality would soon become involvement. There would be no other choices, distasteful as that might be.

After working for Wettergren's Dairy for over ten months, Bill was notified that the owner had decided to cut back on the dairy herd and would be able to manage the milking operation with just family help. His sons aged fourteen and fifteen were pressed into service, and once again Bill was without a job.

When John heard of Bill's latest set-back he suggested that Bill go back to Iowa with him when it was time to pick corn. Bill jumped at the chance to make some money before the opportunity was gone in the advancing winter weather. This fill-in employment would help even though it was not permanent.

Each day that Bill was out in the cold October weather picking corn, he deliberated other job possibilities over and over in his mind. It made no sense to him to keep bounding back and forth between one rural job after the other with no promise of advancement or permanency. He was already nineteen years old and had been a "working man" since he was fourteen. Was he going to live his life as his father had, moving from farm to farm, working at a different job every few years with nothing much to show for his labors except an aching back and calloused hands?

Bill thought back to his CCC days when he almost decided to take an exam to join the Navy. He had gone to Seattle for a weekend and noticed several sailors standing in front of a recruitment office. They struck up a conversation with him and he was interested to hear what they had to say about Navy life. At that time he was too young to be allowed to sign up without permission from his parents, so he dismissed the thought of joining then. Maybe now was the time to explore this possibility further. What did he have to lose? The Navy was a regular job, the pay wasn't bad, and he'd be provided with clothing. The possibility of seeing what lay on the other side of the ocean intrigued him also. All his life he had subconsciously felt the draw of the ocean; a subtle feeling almost as mysterious as the pull of the moon on the tides as the waters washed back and forth on shorelines all over the earth.

Yet he was not unaware of what was going on in the world at the time. Would America soon be called to war? Perhaps it would be best to already be in the military, serving his country if war did become definite. It would be good to make those choices personally before they were made for him.

By early November all the corn crop had been picked, and Bill came back home after a stop in Mankato at the Navy recruitment office. He had signed his name on the enlistment papers and became a member of the U. S. Navy! All that was left to do was the dreaded chore of telling his parents of his decision.

The ride home from Mankato never seemed so long as Bill mulled over how he would relate his news to the family. John had arrived home earlier by a couple hours and when he heard Bill drive in the yard; he met him at the door, giving him a hug and a wink that said he already knew about Bill's enlistment in the Navy. The brothers were very close and usually sensed what the other was going to do long before they knew for sure themselves!

Bill was pretty certain that Lars would share his sense of adventure. After all, as a young man, Lars had left his homeland and journeyed thousands of mile away from Sweden. He had been supportive when Bill left for CCC camp; reacting just as Bill thought he would. It was no surprise to Bill when upon sharing this most recent plan, Lars immediately slapped Bill on the back, hugged him close and wished him well in the new venture.

Sharing the news with his mother was harder for Bill. In the five months since the birth of Katrina, she had not returned to being the cheerful, loving woman that Bill knew as Mom. She was silent most of the time now; seldom smiled and barely went through the motions of caring for the latest baby. Bill was concerned that she would break into uncontrollable sobbing when he told her that he would be leaving home again. As it turned out, Karin just could not find words to say to her son that day and her only reaction was tear-filled eyes as she gazed beyond Bill's shoulder after hugging him closely for a moment.

Jana and Lorraine were excited to hear what Bill told them, but he felt that they didn't really grasp what this meant. Jana was old enough to understand that he would be gone from home for a long time. Lorraine was simply excited to know that he would be dressed in a "sailor suit" as she had seen in pictures. Karl had been gone from home for several years and would get the news of Bill's enlistment from Lars, probably long after Bill already left.

Bill decided to personally visit Anna and Mel to tell them. They were all caught up in the excitement of a newborn baby daughter and Bill was anxious to see them and his firstborn niece. He made plans to stop by their apartment the next morning.

But before going to see his big sister and her family, he still had one last evening at home with the rest of the Perssons. This morning before he left for work, Lars put on a pot of soup. Simple meals were all that Karin could manage to get on the table. Supper usually consisted of either soup or sandwiches made from some kind of left-over roast. Other times it might be fried potatoes and fried eggs that Lars prepared when he returned home in the evening.

Jana was a big help in the kitchen and Lorraine helped by setting the table. Little Katrina gazed on the activity from her blanketed spot on the floor, amusing herself with spoons and a rag ball.

As the family sat down to eat, Bill gazed on each wondering how they would get along once he left on this new adventure. He comforted himself in the fact that they seemed to manage when he was away at CCC Camp and again each time he found himself working away from home for weeks at a time. They would do just fine he was sure. If only Karin could get over her "sadness."

When the meal was over, Bill pushed his chair away from the table and announced that he would take clean up duty tonight. "Come on, John, let's get at the dishwashing," he said to his brother. "When did I sign up for this?" John protested. "Won't hurt a bit," Bill replied. "The sooner we get done, the sooner we can see what's happening downtown," Bill added.

Lars and Karin found comfortable spots in the living room, each in their favorite rocking chair; Jana and Lorraine were soon were involved in the evening radio episode of "The Green Hornet." Katrina was asleep on Karin's lap before Bill and John had finished their work in the kitchen.

As quickly as they could put on a clean shirt and run a brush through their hair, the brothers raced out the door to see what was going on in town that evening. Bill was anxious to see if any of his friends were around town. He wanted one more chance to see some of them before leaving for the Navy in just a few days. The short drive into town went by quickly and soon John was guiding the car to a halt on Main Street. They decided on the ride into town that they would check out the bowling alley first. As soon as they pulled open the door of the building, wafts of cigarette smoke drifted into the street and they could see inside that two or more of their buddies were enjoying a loud and animated round of bowling. Fred Schmidt had just gotten a strike and was prancing around like he was the king of everything.

"Hey there, Pro," Bill called out. "How's it going?"

"Did you see that one?" asked Fred. "I am the best in the league now!" he announced to anybody within earshot.

With just three more frames to finish, the game quickly was over. Fred told Bill and John that he and Don Mueller planned to drive to Mankato to go roller skating now and asked if they would care to come along too.

Fred mentioned that Evelyn, Katie and Grace were going to meet them at the roller rink so Bill and John decided that sounded like fun too. Evelyn and Fred were still a couple but no wedding plans had been shared with their friends as yet. The social activities of the group were still just a number of friends gathering to share an activity; regardless of whether they went to a movie, roller skating or to a barn dance.

Once the boys arrived at the roller rink, they immediately got their skates on and started around the rink. Soon they found the three girls sitting in a booth having soft drinks. All six began animated conversation about what everyone was doing and did they have any special plans for the future. At such a perfect opening in the conversation, Bill announced to the group that he had joined the Navy and would be leaving for basic training in a few days. Everyone wished him well and shared in his excitement about his coming adventure.

In a short time the music began again and the whole group started skating around the rink once more. Suddenly Bill was surprised to see

Rosemarie Swanson, arm in arm with a tall, red-headed young man. As soon as she spotted Bill, she waved in recognition. Quickly moving to where Bill was skating, she blurted out "Hi, do you remember me, Bill?" Before he could answer, she said, "Rosemarie Swanson. You used to work for my Dad." Oh yes, he did remember Rosemarie Swanson and the crush she had on him when he worked for the Swansons. The conversation was short and soon Bill left Rosemarie with her date and rejoined his group. His only comment was that "some things never change!" Katie teased that soon he would not only have a girl in every port, he'd have one in roller rinks all over the world too! Much too soon the last skate was announced and the group went their separate way home again. It was a fun evening and Bill was glad that he had a chance to say goodbyes to some of his friends before his Navy years began.

The next morning when John left for work, Bill rode into town with him, stopping at Mel and Anna's apartment. He wanted to get there early enough to see Mel before he left for the day and luckily Mel was just coming out the door when Bill arrived. They exchanged friendly handshakes and Mel wished Bill the best of luck before he had hurried off. Anna stood just inside the tiny apartment holding her baby daughter. Bill took the baby from her and found a comfortable spot on the sofa to get acquainted with his new niece.

"Oh, Annie," Bill began. "I hope that someday you can share the same thrill as I do now when I will watch you hold my child." Anna found herself without words. She sat down next to Bill and encircled him and her baby in her arms. She hoped Bill knew how much she loved him and how worried she was to have him going off to unknown places so far from home.

CHAPTER 8:

ANCHORS AWEIGH

Early in the morning of December 14, 1938 Bill boarded the train for the trip that would take him to Great Lakes Naval Training Station where he would begin his Navy adventure. There were several other passengers also boarding that day; an elderly couple who climbed into the train ever so slowly and a young woman with two small children. The smallest of the children seemed to be about three years old, a boy whose short legs strained against the steep climb up the steps. Bill stepped forward to give the child a lift up into the train and the mother turned and expressed her thanks to Bill. "My pleasure, Ma'am," he answered, "big steps are hard with short legs."

After a final wave to Lars who stood watching him leave, Bill settled into the first available seat, several rows behind the young family. In a short time, the train slowly eased out of the station, traveling northward first to Minneapolis, then southeast towards Chicago. The Minnesota countryside was white with several inches of snow that had recently fallen, giving fairyland beauty to all views from the train windows.

After three stops in small towns along the way, the train arrived in Minneapolis around ten o'clock. The elderly couple who had gotten on the train in Le Sueur inched their way along the aisle to get off at their stop and other travelers joined those passengers already on board. Soon the train gathered speed, traveling across Wisconsin towards Chicago. Bill wondered to himself if this was the same route in reverse that his family had traveled when they first came to America.

The conductor called out in a loud voice, "Next stop, Rockford," as the young mother and her children were passing by Bill's seat, returning to the car after a trip to the restroom. The little boy recognized Bill and climbed up into the empty seat next to him before his mother could stop him.

"I want to sit here, Mama," he announced. Bill had just finished a cheese sandwich and had started to peel an orange when the child sat down. "If you don't mind, ma'am, it's all right with me," Bill offered. Soon Bill and the little boy were sharing juicy sections of the orange together as the train rumbled along the way.

Again the conductor walked through the passenger cars announcing, "Next stop, Chicago." All the passengers began gathering their belongings as they prepared to depart the train. Bill proceeded down the steps to the platform, turning in time to say farewell to his small seat partner who had rejoined his mother.

"Bye Max," he said to the little boy. "Maybe someday we can share another orange," he added.

Then turning, he looked to find the right gate that would lead him to another train and his final destination, Great Lakes Naval Training Station. He soon found Gate 5 with a sign that read "Great Lakes, Illinois." Heading in the same direction were a group of other young men, their faces full of anticipation and excitement about where they were going and at the same time worried eyes betrayed the fearful feelings they tried to hide against the unknown. Soon all were on board, heading towards their final destination.

The next few days went by in a blur. Bill found himself busy from morning until evening learning as much as he could possibly absorb about his new life in the Navy. His first long letter home was written to Karl explaining what he had experienced so far.

***

U.S.Naval Training Station
Great Lakes, Ill
Sun. Dec 18, 1938 8:30PM
Hello Karl,

I've got so much to write about that I don't know how to start, but I'll make a stab at it anyhow. First I'll tell you a few of the rules. The rules they have around here would fill a book, and a big book at that.

The primary rules are as follows: No glass containers allowed in camp, ink, hair oil, etc, no wooden matches, no civilian clothes. No smoking after 8:00 PM. No talking after lights out. Lights out 9:30 PM. Take a shower every day. Shave, brush teeth, wash underwear, leggings, socks, towel, shine shoes every day. Salute all officers, wear overcoat buttoned, wear leggings properly laced. We sleep in hammocks, these have to be made up in military fashion every morning, wash bed clothes and uniform every week. March in military order to mess hall, chapel service, moving picture show. Fall out in twos for drill practice, clothes have to be rolled and tied with cord in a certain manner. Sea-bag inspection, every Sat. Barracks cleaned every morning, and thousand and one other rules and regulations.

Fifteen fellows in our bunch got here Wednesday morning. Took some more strenuous physical exams, then received our issue of clothing. We sure got a mess of clothes to take care of. Every piece of clothing including shoes, rubbers, leggings, etc. is stenciled with our name. The blues are stenciled in white, the whites stenciled in black.

Spent all day Thursday learning how to roll clothes. Boy my fingers were wore before night. There are several hundred apprentice seamen in camp. They come from every part of U.S.

Floors aren't called floors here. They are "decks". Friday is field day in the Navy, in other words, cleaning day. Everything has to be cleaned spic and span for Saturday inspection by the "Gold Braids"(big shots). Spent all day Friday washing decks, scrubbing stairs and cleaning windows. Got my regulation hair cut; that is they cut all my hair off. Everybody gets one. Then to add insult to injury, the son-of-a-guns charge us 15 cents for the job. Took two shots in the arms, have some more coming.

We are made prisoners as soon as we arrive here. There is a high steel fence around the place. The gates are guarded by "gobs" carrying rifles. No one leaves camp for 3 weeks. No visitors allowed. The time goes by bells here. It is 6 bells now, 3 O'clock by civilian time. Navy time is called by the hour; hence 1:00 P.M is 13:00; 9:30 PM is 21:30.

I'm learning how to signal with flags. One signal stands for each different letter of the alphabet. It's called the semaphore.

We didn't get everything here and we had to buy a lot of things at the ships service store such as: The Blue Jackets Manual which cost 1.60, shoe polish, razor blades, horsehide mitts, laundry and toilet soap, tooth paste, shaving cream and all other toilet articles and stationery. Have to buy our uniforms and everything from now on. I've spent about five bucks already.

You mentioned something about sending me the dough you owe me, well fellow, I sure could use those 4 bucks right now. You can have my grey suit and that CCC mackinaw of mine if you send that money to me. Don't use any of my other clothes though unless I write and tell you. I'll be home for leave in March if I don't get too many de-merits. Tell dad he can have that blue plaid jacket of mine for paying the C.O.D charges on the clothes I sent home. I won't need it anymore.

John wanted to buy my rain coat. Tell him he can have it for $2.00 if he wants it. Ask him to send the dough as soon as he can. How's the sawing coming along?

Running out of space here so I'll have to sign off for this time, hope everybody in good health at home. I'm in tip-top shape.

Xmas greetings to all. Adios, and may we meet again. As ever, Bill
Co. #31 U.S. Naval Training Station, Great Lakes, Illinois

***

Mail call was eagerly anticipated by all the young recruits. As they worked through the drills of learning new navy skills, they scarcely had time to give much thought to how they felt about their decision to join the Navy and most fell into their hammocks in the evening too tired to stay awake for any length of time. Yet all thoughts did turn to home often as they wondered about their families, what their siblings might be doing, what was going on in the old hometown. When a letter came from home, they poured over the words whether it might be a scrawled word or two or a longer letter with all kinds of details. They felt reconnected again when news came from home.

Bill tried to take time to answer those letters that came to him. Shortly after receiving a letter from Karl, he responded back to his brother asking him to remind "mother to send the clipping from the News Herald about when I left for the Navy. And you can use the battery from my car if you need it."

Christmas of 1938 was pretty much a day the same as any other at Great Lakes, the exception being that drilling was cut short. The cooks prepared turkey and dressing for the holiday meal doing their best to duplicate what "Mom used to make." Later in the afternoon the recruits passed their free time with furious games of ping-pong or by challenging any takers to a game of basketball.

Soon the month on the calendar read "January" and the year 1939 began with Bill writing home to share details of his life in the Navy. His response to Karin began by telling her how pleased he was to have received a letter from her.

***

U.S. Naval Tra. Sta.
Great Lakes, Ill.
January 13, 1939
Dear Mom,
Got your letter yesterday, was very glad to hear from you. It's so seldom I get a letter from anybody that when I do get one I read it over and over.

Haven't much to write about, just the usual routine in camp. Taking orders, drilling and catching a lot of heck wherever a fellow turns.

Yesterday we moved from the detention camp (C camp) over to the main camp commonly known as "Paradise," but it isn't what the name implies, in fact it's just the opposite. A fellow can't make one false move without someone jumping on his neck, everything has to be perfect and on the second.

One fellow just got out of the brig today. He was locked up three days on bread and water because he fell asleep on watch. They've got a million rules and regulations; if we break just one it's too bad. But of course they have to have discipline in any military organization or it would be an awful mess. They have the de-merit system here. For every 25 demerits we lose a day leave at the end of training. Here are some things we can get demerits for, profane language 5, dropping rifle 3, button missing on uniform 2, dirty clothes in bag 2, wet clothes 3, talking after lights out 3, disobeying orders 15, not in full uniform 3. There are 56 different rules we can get demerits for, so you see it wouldn't take very long to get 25 and lose a day.

Still I'm not sorry I joined, we have a lot of fun too. I like to be with a bunch of boys.

Took the swimming test today. I only swam 40 yards but I guess I'll improve with practice. Have a large indoor pool, also a gym where we can box, wrestle and run track. They charge 25 cents for roller-skating in the armory. Shows twice a week. Dances held every 2 weeks; they "import" the girls from Chicago for the dances.

There are 300 men in each barracks so you can just about imagine how quiet and peaceful it is all day. Each man makes just a little more noise than the other. Gosh I guess I never will get used to sleeping in a hammock. In the detention camp we slept 4 feet above the deck. Here in Paradise the hammocks are 8 feet above the deck so if a guy rolls out in his sleep he has an awful long way to fall.

We get $6 a month; get paid on the 5 and 20th of each month. They hold back $15 a month of our pay so we'll have something to go home on when we get leave.

The last couple days we have been drilling the "extended order" bayonet assault, squad rushes, platoon movements, etc.

I'm glad to hear everyone is in good health at home. I'm feeling fine. Sent a letter and picture to Otto the other day. Got a letter from Katie Schmidt, outside of that I don't know much about what's happening around Le Sueur.

Will have to close as it's soon time for chow, if I'm late at the mess hall I'll get a couple hours extra duty. *There sure is a long line of men going to chow, have to wait in line behind several hundred guys, I don't like that but it's all in the game.*

We got out of our quarantine yesterday, now another company has the measles and they are locked up in their barracks. Well goodbye, be sure to write soon. Love to all at home, Bill

P.S. The weather is pretty changeable here, today it snowed. But it doesn't get very cold because we are close to Lake Michigan.

***

The days of boot camp passed with one learning experience after the other and by February 14, 1939 Bill mused to himself that this "ordeal" was half over. Before long he could allow himself to get excited about getting leave and having the chance to go home again for a few days. A change from training, drill and discipline would be good. While he did enjoy his new found friends and learning together about Navy ways, there was discontent in life too as he mentioned in a letter home that said; "A day in the Navy is like Sunday on the farm. Always some irksome job to do!"

One irksome job was working in the galley. Dishing up chow for hundreds of sailors was quite a job, not to mention washing food trays and cleaning up the area. But he took the galley rotation in stride, knowing that just around the corner would be some other equally bothersome duty. One just did the duty of the day as it came around.

The announcement that trade school examinations would be given near the end of February caught Bill's interest. He thought that the opportunity to learn a trade would really benefit him once he was back in civilian life, yet he was hesitant to take the test because of his limited education. He would find himself competing with high school graduates and others who had some college experience. How could a grade school graduate compete with that? He decided that his best chances were to wait until he could learn some trade first hand while serving aboard ship.

One day he got the welcome news telling him that Lars had paid off the balance owed on his car and Bill considered the possibility of trying to sell that car when he got home on leave. He thought that it probably be just as well to do that since all the car did was depreciate in value as it sat in the shed while he was away. Maybe his brother Karl would want to buy it.

So many nights just before sleep, thoughts about home and family came to Bill as he twisted and turned to find a comfortable position in his hammock before eventually drifting off to sleep. He wondered if Uncle Sander might decide to drive up to see him at Great Lakes. After all, Genoa, Illinois wasn't that far away. Was Pa still working on the WPA? And Uncle Otto's return letter was short, but then there's not much to write about while in prison.

Towards the end of February, the flu ran rampant through the naval barracks. Unfortunately Bill did a rotation with that "duty" also. He was taken by ambulance to the hospital where he found himself lying in a hospital bed while on a clear liquid diet for four days. After a few more recovery days at the hospital, he grew tired of this "soft life" and became anxious to get back to work again. On the positive side of things, he was still able to draw his pay while being sick, not unlike his days of working as a hired man for some "penny-pinching farmer who would only pay you when you were on your feet." This Navy life did have some advantages.

After the hospital stay, Bill reported back to duty to find that his new rotation would involve nighttime guarding of the "dipsy dumpsters", garbage cans positioned by the side of the parade grounds. Winter had not yet released its grip on Great Lakes Naval Station and it was cold, snowy, and dark outside. But at least he had pleasant company while on this duty, someone that he had met briefly the summer before joining when he was working back home at the canning factory. His marching companion was from Hinkley, MN and now they found themselves back together, once again proof to Bill that this "old USA isn't so big after all."

Then at last the big day came and boot camp leave was granted; all would have ten glorious days to see family and friends back in the old home town! All the recruits were in high spirits as they boarded the train that carried them to Chicago. They happily called to their buddies to have safe traveling and good times with their loved ones. Since nobody had been able to leave camp after arriving there on December 14, their release was very exciting, almost like the last day of the school year with the entire summer ahead, to enjoy at will.

The train ride from Great Lakes depot to Union Station in Chicago went by quickly. Once there, large groups of sailors departed that train and scattered across the station to begin their search for the gate number that directed them to where they would board the next train towards home. Bill and about eight other men in blue noted that Gate #3 was where they would find the next train leaving for Minneapolis. They discovered that other passengers were already boarding and they needed to hurry along too. After a quick stop at the restroom and an even quicker stop to buy candy bars, they were ready to get on board for the next leg of their homeward journeys.

As Bill was stepping into the first car with available seating, a small boy's voice called out, "Hi Bill! You look different!"

Bill could not imagine that he would be traveling once again with Max, the tow-headed youngster that shared an orange with him last

December as Bill traveled to Chicago. But there was Max, scrambling to sit down in the same seat with Bill. Quickly his mother came along and tried to reseat the youngster with herself and her other child. Max persisted and announced that he wanted to sit with Bill.

"It's all right with me, Ma'am. I'd like to renew this friendship if you will let him sit with me," Bill said to the young woman. So the two "friends" were together again; this time without an orange. Soon Max began happily unwrapping one of Bill's Hershey bars and sporting Bill's sailor cap on his head. Then came all the questions; why is your hair short, why are you wearing that scratchy suit, where did you get the funny necktie, what's in that white bag under the seat??? Patiently Bill answered his little "friend's" questions and on the train ride to Minnesota, life was just about perfect for Max!

While Bill sat in his seat listening to the happy prattle of Max, he gazed out the window, watching the passing scenery as the train traveled the return miles to Minnesota. Most of the snows of December had melted into miles of March mud! There were so many changes in the look of the land, the milder temperatures of spring weather; not to mention the changes in himself! He was no longer a young man uncertain of his future. He was positive now after these past few weeks in boot camp training, that his decision to join the Navy was right for him. He could hardly wait to share these good feelings with his family and friends at home.

As the train pulled into the station in Le Sueur, Bill noted a young father standing on the platform. Max spotted the man also and excitedly called out, "Momma, momma. Daddy is here!"

The train lumbered to a screechy stop as Max' family and Bill began walking towards the door where the conductor stood ready to help everyone down the steps. The young family greeted each other with hugs; and with one last wave to Bill, Max clambered into their waiting car. Bill looked around to see if Lars was there to pick him up, then after a few minutes he hoisted his sea bag onto his shoulder and began to walk towards downtown, hopeful of finding someone who might give him a ride those couple miles south of town to home. Main Street was nearly deserted by now, the stores were all closed and just a handful of cars were on the street.

As Bill neared Bridge Street, the honking horn of a truck startled him. He turned to see Cy Gunders, who was heading homeward towards his farm. Cy called out to Bill, "Hey there, sailor man, do you need a ride?"

"Hello Cy," Bill answered. "I don't know where my Dad is. He was going to meet me at the depot. "Well, climb in," Cy said, "I'll take you home."

After a few more minutes of catch up conversation, Cy turned into the drive to the Persson place. There was Lars in the farmyard, struggling in lantern light to change the flat tire on Bill's old Chevy sedan.

"Hello, Dad," Bill called out. Lars stood up at the sound of Bill's voice and turned to see his handsome young sailor son standing there. Cy had turned his truck around and shouted a quick hello and goodbye as he headed out the drive again.

"Thanks a million, Cy," Bill called out as the truck disappeared from sight. "Bill, I'm so sorry I wasn't there to meet you at the train," Lars began. "I sure didn't need a flat tire when I was going to pick you up. My old Ford isn't running. It needs an overhaul and I don't have the money right now. So I've been driving your Chevy. And now a flat tire!"

"It's all right, Dad," Bill answered. "I'm here now and it's so good to be home again," he continued. After a firm hug to each other, both walked into the house.

At the sound of Bill's voice, Jana and Lorraine raced into the kitchen, arms wide open ready for hugs from their brother. And soon, after hearing the happy voices greeting each other, Karin entered the room, carrying Katrina. "Oh, my goodness, Bill, you are home,"

Karin began. "Let me put the little one down so that I can give you a proper hug."

But Bill did not wait and hurried across the room to embrace both his mother and his little sister at once. "How's that for a proper hug?" he asked his mother.

Once the hellos and hugs were over, Karin passed Katrina to Jana and began pulling items from the ice-box to prepare supper for Bill. Soon a plate of fried potatoes and eggs was placed on the table and Bill sat down to this homely, home-cooked feast.

By the time he'd finished supper, the effects of his long day of travel became evident in Bill. The conversation continued about his Navy adventures as the family found seats in the living room, but about a half hour later Bill announced that he was really tired and wanted to go to bed.

"Of course you're tired," remarked Lars. "You can tell us more tomorrow." And so, after a quick goodnight to all, Bill found his way to the bedroom he once shared with John. He crawled into bed, relishing the solid feel of a mattress once more, a welcome change from the hammock at Great Lakes. He was asleep in no time.

Morning was announced much too early, by an errant young rooster testing his new found crowing ability. Bill sat up rubbed his eyes, trying to acclimate himself to his surroundings. He got out of bed, and rummaged through the closet in search of some civilian clothes. He found a pair of pants and a shirt that belonged to John and put them on because he didn't think his brother would mind if he borrowed them. After dressing, he padded into the kitchen in his bare feet. Lars had made coffee and poured a cup for Bill. Before long, two groggy sisters joined the group in the kitchen. Lars poured each a bowl of cereal and the girls sat in silence, munching on their breakfast.

"This certainly is a lively group," Bill offered. In unison, the sisters just rolled their eyes, indicating that it was still much too early for talking.

Lars turned to Bill and said, "Maybe you could take the girls to school today for me. Alvin Jensen will be here to pick me up soon to ride to work with him. Then you can use your car to visit people in town and bring the girls home again after school." At the prospect of not having to walk home after school, both sisters immediately perked up and eagerly finished breakfast and hurried back to the bedroom to finish getting ready for their day. Bill agreed that his father's suggestion was a good one and he went to find his shoes and a jacket to prepare for the drive to town.

The next sound heard was the tooting of the horn on Alvin's truck, telling Lars that it was time to leave for work. He hurried out the door, calling a quick "goodbye-I'll be home at 6:00" to anyone who might hear him. Soon another morning sound was heard from Karin's bedroom as Katrina squalled that she was wet and hungry! Karin pulled on her housedress and toted the baby into the kitchen after getting her changed for the day. She poured herself a cup of coffee, then retreated into the living room to her rocking chair where she sat down to begin feeding Katrina.

"I think I'll stop by to see Anna after I drop the girls at school," Bill said to his mother through the doorway. "That's a good idea, son. I know she is anxious to see you too," Karin answered. "Bye, Mom," Bill went on. "I'll see you later this afternoon."

Jana and Lorraine ran out the door ahead of Bill and soon the three siblings were on their way to town. Upon arriving at school, the girls quickly jumped out of the car, calling their goodbyes as they hurried into the building.

Bill turned the car around and headed back through downtown, then up the hill to the house where his sister Anna, her husband and daughter were living in the second floor apartment. It was past 8:30 now and Bill knew that Mel had left for work already when he didn't see the old black Ford in the driveway.

He climbed up the outside stairway and rapped on the door. Soon Anna answered his knock and cried out in surprise to see him at her door. "Hello, there little brother," Anna said regaining her composure. Bill stepped in and gave his sister a warm hug that spoke volumes of how much he cared for her and how glad he was to see her again. Soon they were happily catching up on each other's news. The visit was cut short by cries from the bedroom. Anna went in, picked up her baby daughter and Bill looked at his little niece exclaiming over how much she had grown during the few months that he was gone.

For about an hour the happy visiting went on, each sharing what was going on in their lives. Bill glanced at his watch and exclaimed that he really should be going as he had several more stops to make. Plans were made for Anna and Mel to join the Persson family two days later on Sunday. Bill explained that Karin had hoped that all of the family could come for dinner and they would also be celebrating Bill's 20ᵗʰ birthday. Anna volunteered that she would plan to bring a cake.

"We'll see you then," Bill said as he opened the door to leave. "I hope that Mom will fix fried chicken. What we get in the Navy is close to fried albatross!"

Back in the car, Bill headed for downtown where he decided to stop in at the drug store. His friend Evelyn worked there and he wanted to see her and learn what was new between her and Fred Schmidt. The two had been going together for nearly a year now and Bill was curious to know if they were talking about marriage. Evelyn looked up from assisting a customer as Bill walked into the store.

"Hi Bill, it's good to see you again. When did you get back," the question came from Evelyn. Bill explained that he'd be home for about ten days and asked if she and Fred like to get together tonight. Plans were set and Bill again got into the car and headed for his next stop, seeing Karl at the farm where he was working. It took about thirty minutes to reach the Bergerstad place, just northwest of St. Peter. When he pulled into the farmyard, the first thing he heard was the sound of the wood splitter, as Karl worked to cut the large logs into cook-stove size.

Bill walked over to where Karl was working and stood there in sight, waiting for Karl to look up and realize that his brother was there. Soon Karl did just that, stopped the rig and immediately shook hands firmly with Bill. Bill extended his mother's Sunday invitation and Karl agreed that he would be there. After a short conversation, Bill again headed down the road. This time his destination was Cleveland and the place where John worked. As he turned into the drive, he was met by a pick-up truck driven by his brother John. John stopped as soon as he realized it was Bill driving the car coming towards him.

"Hey there, brother Bill," John shouted. "Nice shirt you have," teased John. Bill smiled back at his brother answering him, "Ya, and it looks better on me too!"

John went on, "I'm on my way into town to buy chicken feed. Why don't you meet me in Cleveland at the café on Main Street and we'll have a sandwich and talk for a while." Bill agreed and within a short time the brothers were happily enjoying a hamburger and sharing news of what was going on in their lives. When they had finished eating, Bill extended his mother's invitation to come for Sunday dinner. John said he would be there. In fact, he would come home on Saturday and they could maybe head to a dance in Mankato or see who was at the roller skating rink.

Having completed the Sunday plans, Bill headed towards Le Sueur. Once back in town, he parked the car on Main Street and got out to walk down the familiar streets of his hometown. This time he went into Nichol's Variety Store just to see if there were any changes there. Of course none were evident. The same items were still in the same arrangements on the same counters. Mr. Nichols was just as terse as ever and Mrs. Nichols was as full of smiles and just as friendly as she always had been. Bill thought back to how she had thoughtfully tied a big red bow on the sled he bought for his little sisters some Christmas' ago.

Bill left Nichol's store and walked on down the street to the hardware store. He had noticed that the old broom standing in the back porch at home was looking pretty worn and he decided to purchase a new one to surprise his mother.

After placing the new broom in the car, he headed towards the elementary school to pick up his sisters. He was surprised how quickly the day had gone. He had seen all his siblings and made plans with them to be at home on Sunday but he still wanted to see as many of his friends as possible and spend some time with them if he could. It was going to be hard to get around to everyone in the short time he had available, but he would do the best that he could.

That night after supper, Fred Schmidt came to pick up Bill. He was going into town to see Evelyn and she, along with several others were all going to the show that night. Bill was so glad to be included in the plans and was excited about seeing his friends again. It really was great to be home and slip back into old times again.

By eleven o'clock on Sunday morning, Karl rolled into the Persson yard in his truck. Bill looked out the bedroom window when he heard the truck and of course he knew right away that it was Karl. By the time Karl climbed down from the cab, Mel and Anna were driving into the yard also. John had come home the day before as planned and was still sleeping at this late hour.

"Come on, John. Get up! You're going to miss dinner if you don't move out of that bed," Bill said to his brother before he walked down the hall to the kitchen. "Hello, everyone," called Bill as he came into the room. Karin had been up since early morning and she'd been busy in the kitchen. The potatoes were boiling in the pot, the chicken was all fried and waiting in the warming oven. Anna had brought a birthday cake as she promised and she set the plate on the side cupboard counter. Soon a sleepy-eyed John joined the group in the kitchen began to add to the happy conversation filling the room.

Jana and Lorraine took the two baby girls into the living room and busied themselves rolling a ball back and forth between the babies. Anna set to work helping her mother get the meal on the table and soon all were saying Grace before digging into the tasty chicken dinner. After the table was cleared and the dishes all washed and put away, Karin announced that she would really like to have a family picture taken now that all her children were home again. It seemed a good idea and the mild March day made it easy for everyone to be outside for a while to take a picture without getting too chilly. After several poses were taken by Mel, the acting photographer, the group came back inside and birthday cake was served. It goes without saying that coffee was served also. Any good Swede is seldom in the kitchen very long without a cup of coffee! Then all joined in singing a boisterous version of Happy Birthday to Bill. It was a memorable day for everyone.

The remaining days of Bill's leave passed by much too quickly for him. Bill was able to enjoy time with his family and also get together with many of his friends while enjoying all the activities they had shared before he enlisted and left home. There was a new girl among the St. Peter group now. Her name was Paula Manley. She had just moved into town and had previously met up with the group at a dance. The second Saturday night of Bill's leave, Bill and John went to another dance at the same ballroom. Paula was there and she and Bill struck up a conversation. Both immediately felt they could become good friends and wondered why they had not met earlier!

Some of Bill's day leave time was spent at home, helping as he could. He was glad that he was able to help a bit with odd jobs around the farm that never seemed to get done while Lars was off to work every day.

Karin seemed unable to complete the household chores also. He did observe that she seemed much happier while he was at home. But Anna had told him about the several times when she came to visit and found Karin just sitting in the rocking chair, staring in space. On another occasion, Anna found Karin in bed in the middle of the afternoon, not dressed for the day and baby Katrina asleep on the floor beside the bed. The "sad time" for Karin was lasting much longer than it had after her previous children were born and all of the family was well aware of the problem.

Even though he was concerned about this, there was nothing that he could do and as the end of his leave time came around, he found himself thinking ahead to his return to Great Lakes. He had thoroughly enjoyed the time at home with his family and friends, but he had made a choice when he enlisted and the Navy was now the most important part of his life. He found himself thinking about his basic training friends and wondering if they felt the same way as he did; anxious to get back to naval regimentation and ready for any adventures that might come to the young recruits.

There had been lots of talk among the men before their leave about what choices they might be allowed once they returned to base. Bill waivered back and forth about the decision of where and how he wanted to serve but finally decided to sign up for duty on a destroyer. He liked the idea of being on a smaller ship; he reasoned that there would be a better chance to know more of the men. Maybe there would be more of a small town feeling instead of the crowded atmosphere aboard one of the larger ships.

A short time after returning to Great Lakes Naval Station, orders came down and on April 18, 1939 Bill was once again traveling by train, this time heading for Norfolk, VA. He had hoped that his shipping out point would allow for a side trip to the World's Fair in New York City, but the Navy had other plans for him and New York City was not a part of it.

Soon after arriving in Norfolk, he was put aboard a light cruiser which then set sail with the rest of a fleet of battle ships, destroyers, cruisers and carriers. Their rendezvous point was "the ditch at Colon", where they would lay at anchor just inside the Canal Zone.

His next letter home described his train journey to the East Coast, his first sailing trip to the Panama Canal and ultimately being assigned to duty aboard the USS Preston.

CHAPTER 9:

USS PRESTON-DD379

(The Preston was a Mahan-class destroyer, built at Mare Island Navy Yard, California and commissioned in 1936. She was armed with a main battery of four-five inch/38 dual-purpose guns, twelve torpedo tubes, seven 20-mm Oberlikon antiaircraft guns and an array of depth charges for use against submarines–Recollections from Ensign Robert B. Reed)

****

Colon, Panama Canal Zone
U.S.S. Preston
April 27, 1939
Dear Mother,
I'm down by the Panama Canal now. But I'll start from the beginning.

Left the training station the 18th. Suppose you got the post card I sent. Traveled through Indiana that night and was in Cincinnati, Ohio the next morning at 7:00 A.M. Laid over there for 3 hrs. and then boarded the train again. Passed through Ohio and West Va. by nightfall. The next morning we were in Virginia. Pulled into Norfolk about 8:00A.M. the 20th. The fleet was ordered to the West Coast, so didn't get a chance to see the World's Fair at New York.

Went aboard ship right away. Was sent on the U.S.S. Concord a light cruiser. Left Norfolk about 10 A.M. the 20th. Traveled south with the whole fleet. Battle ships, destroyers, cruisers, and aircraft carriers. Sure are a lot of ships in this navy.

Only went about 12 knots an hr. all the way down. Went past Cuba and Hispaniola. Finally got to the canal after 6 ½ long days. Got here yesterday. Are now anchored in the bay on the north end of the ditch at Colon.

Was transferred to my own ship yesterday afternoon. The U. S.S. Preston. It's a destroyer, one of the lightest ships in the fleet. Carries a crew of about 150 men. Pretty crowded. It's about 3 yrs. old. She bobs around like a cork, when the sea gets a little rough.

I used to think that it was hot in the summertime back in Minn. But even the weather we had there during threshing time was only lukewarm compared to this country. I've got the most beautiful case of sunburn I've ever had. We sleep in triple bunks, and it's about as cool as an oven. This ship is all steel and iron, even the decks. So you can imagine how hot it is when the sun beats down on it all day. Can hardly walk on the decks even with shoes on.

They really work us on this "tin can." Spent all forenoon washing the hull and painting her. This afternoon I washed grey work on the super structure. Not much time to lay around in the navy. Call a fellow any time of the day or night to help lower or raise a boat, or stand a four-hr. watch. The trip was far from a pleasure cruise on the way down. Ran into some pretty rough waters at times too.

We are getting ready to shove off now at about 8 P.M. Go through the canal tonight. Think we will lay at anchor on the other side, at Balboa for 3 or 4 days. Might get liberty for a few hrs. tomorrow to go ashore.

I'd give an eyetooth right now, just to have some good solid land under my feet. Haven't been ashore since we left Norfolk, Virginia.

They have movies aboard ship almost every night if a fellow cares to stand on deck and watch them. After we leave the Canal Zone we go to South America, across the equator to the country of Equador. After that we return to the home base at San Diego, Cal. which will probably be some time yet.

I bought an Elgin wristwatch at Chicago one Sat. when I went down there. Bought an Eastman folding camera at Cincinnati, Ohio during the layover on the train. But aren't allowed to have a camera on ship so had to check it in. Can use it on liberty parties. Have seen some new country and an awful lot of water in the little distance I have gone. Some 3, 300 miles so far, more or less from Great L. Will go about 1000 miles to Equador, South America, and around 4,000 miles back to San Diego, so I've barely got a good start yet.

Coming down on the Concord it was pretty crowded. About 600 men aboard her. So had to sleep wherever we could find room to swing a hammock. Slept on the deck most nights.

Wear white uniforms in tropical climates. Get laundry done on this ship for $2.00 a month and it sure is worth it cause it's a hard job to wash clothes every night after work. Am getting $36 a month now since I passed my seaman second class test.

All water used has to be distilled from ocean water, so we have to be careful how much we use taking showers, etc. Guess I'll have to close now as we soon will weigh anchor and get underway. Will write more when I get back to California.

Hope everyone at home is feeling O.K. I'm top-notch shape. Except for being a little scorched.

Some of the recruits got pretty seasick coming through the Atlantic and Caribbean seas. Haven't been sick yet but suppose I have mine coming.

Please write soon. I'll get the letter as soon as I get back to the States. Use this address:

William Persson S-2-C
U.S.S. Preston- 379
San Diego, California

Well so long and best wishes to all the family. "I'll be with you when the roses bloom again."

Sincerely, your son, Bill

***

The Preston sailed into the port of San Diego on May 17, 1939. After 4000 miles of ocean between Equador and California, the sailors were glad to view the sight of Point Loma lighthouse as it stood welcoming the fleet back home to the USA again. The process of lashing the Preston to another destroyer was completed quickly and once the ship was secured, the sailors anxiously awaited permission to go ashore and enjoy the sensation of solid ground under their feet again.

***

U.S. S. Preston

May 20, 1939

Dear Mother,

Guess it's about time for me to drop a line or two now that I have some time off. Haven't had a chance to get around to it before as we just got back from South America a couple days ago.

Well, I've had a little taste of the real navy now. Have traveled some 7,000 miles since I left Great Lakes in just about a month.

Was just wondering if you got the letter I sent from Panama. Was hoping you would write and I would have gotten the letter when I came back here, but suppose you thought I would be in So. America longer than I was. We only stayed there about six days. Sure was a long tiresome trip but interesting just the same. But the terrible heat in the Canal Zone and in S. A. was just about enough to kill a fellow.

The letter I sent from Panama I think I wrote while en-route on the Caribbean Sea so will continue from there. Took 6 ½ days to go from Norfolk to Colon. Only made about 12 knots an hour all the way down. Got there the 26th and left for Equador the morning of the 29th after going through the canal. Took from 9:00 in the evening till 5:00 o'clock the next morning to go through. Had to work all night handling ropes going through the locks so didn't get any sleep that night. There are about

12 locks to go through. They lashed 2 destroyers together and put four through a lock at a time so you see these locks are pretty big.

I'm on a destroyer now, which is one of the smallest, fastest ships the navy has. Is 341 ft. long and 34 ft. across. Carries a crew of 150 men. Is used for torpedo offensive and carries 5" guns for defensive. A battle ship has 14" & 16" guns.

As I said we left the 29th of April from the Canal and arrived at our destination the morning of May 2nd. Had to go up a river for 50 miles to get to the city we visited. A sailor who has never crossed the equator is called a "pollywog." One who has, is known as a "shellback." When we crossed the equator we pollywogs were initiated by the shellbacks (ones who had been across before and were aboard) and they really initiated us. Used grease, tar, flour, electricity and everything else they could think of. Took me 2 hrs. of scrubbing with lava soap and kerosene before I looked like anything human again. We were given diplomas after that to certify we had been across. Am sending mine so you can see what it looks like but wish you would send it back to me again because if I ever go across again I'll have to have it or take another initiation.

Had three half- day liberties in Guayaqil, had a lot of fun, but the people there speak Spanish so couldn't very well speak to them. Used sign language and got along pretty good. Exchanged our American dollars for their money to buy stuff. An American dollar is worth 14 sucres and 50 centavos. So the sailors were all flashing rolls of 5 sucre bills around. Everything costs a lot more there than in the U.S. Except fruit which can be bought for little or nothing. I almost gorged myself eating bananas and oranges. This was a so-called good-will tour to promote good feeling between the two nations.

Monday morning the 8th of May we weighed anchor and left for San Diego. Had fairly nice weather coming back again. The trip back was uneventful. Took nine days to get back doing 15 knots per hr. Sure is a long time to see nothing but water day & night.

The weather here in California is wonderful, warm days and cool nights. We wear blue uniforms here. Wore whites in S.A.

The fleet is in now so there are almost as many sailors as there are civilians in San Diego. It has a population of about 200,000. Guayaquil had about 175.000. A common working man gets 4 sucres a day there in Equador. (29 cents) Most of the people are poor in that country, just live in poverty. Worse than I've seen in any North American city I've been in, but they all seem carefree and happy. Glad to get back to the old U.S.

I'm in the deck force now but am going to try to get in the "black-gang" (engineers force) soon, as a fellow has a better chance to get a rating there. Bought some souvenirs in Equador and am sending some home. Just cheap stuff but thought you" like to have it just as a remembrance. Will send it as soon as I get a hold of a box and get to the post office. Handkerchief apiece for the kids, a scarf for you and one for Anna. Sox for Pa, a cigarette case for John and a belt for Karl.

I've been ashore twice in Diego so far. Think I will like it O.K. here. They sure know how to charge the sailors for everything we buy though. Lot higher than Minnesota.

Think we'll be here most of the time now, but probably will go to 'Frisco to the fair later on in the summer. Might go to Hawaii yet this year, don't know yet.

Got a letter from Sander the other day when we came in.

Hope this finds everyone at home O.K. I'm top-notch.

Will have to quit now and tell you more about it next time. Will be looking for an answer soon. Best regards to the whole family.

Your son, Bill

***

May of 1939 was warm and pleasant in small town Minnesota. Some of the early gardeners were already enjoying fresh lettuce and crispy radishes. School would soon end for the year and the children were counting the days until summer vacation. May in Europe was warm and pleasant also but anything but peaceful. Hitler had taken over Czechoslovakia and was also occupying Bohemia and Moravia. Germany and Russia had signed a non-aggression pact with the condition that Russia would take over Estonia, Latvia and Lithuania. So while the Persson family enjoyed peaceful, warm spring days, it was not so in other parts of the world. America read about or listened to world news every day but seemed only politely interested in what was going on.

A package from Bill arrived close to the end of the month. True to words in his previous letter, he found a box and mailed home the small souvenir items that he had purchased in Equador. When Jana and Lorraine came home from school one day, Karin told them that a box from Bill had come in the morning mail.

"Mama, what is in the package for us," Lorraine excitedly asked. "Let's take a look," Karin answered. Both girls soon held the hand-sewn handkerchiefs that Bill had sent.

"Oh, Mom," Jana exclaimed. "I think we should put these away to keep forever. They are just too beautiful to use."

Karin agreed and the handkerchiefs and her scarf were carefully folded and placed in the dresser drawer to only be admired once or twice but never used. The rest of the gifts to the family were admired when claimed, the only difference being that Lars put his socks on right away, John lit up a cigarette with the lighter and Karl wore the hand tooled belt every day until he later swapped civilian clothes for a US Army uniform.

***

U.S.S.Preston
San Diego, Calif.
June 7, 1939
Dear Mom,
Received your letter a couple days ago. Also got the first one you sent, when I first came here to this port. Haven't very much to write about,

because it seems whenever a person is, work becomes a routine and one day is quite a bit like the next.

Our division of destroyers have been in port since we got back from South America. Tied up to the destroyer tender the U.S.S. Dobbin.

Monday the 5th we weighed anchor and went on a short cruise for a few miles out at sea. Had direction finding practice, also depth sounding and gun training. Anchored out in the ocean Monday & Tuesday nights and came back to San Diego this afternoon. Guess that's what the work will be mostly this summer. Short cruises for torpedo schools and submarine sounding. We're supposed to dry-dock at Bremerton, Wash. Next January. A ship is dry-docked about once every 18 months.

Seems kind of strange to live on a ship all the time. Even in port we're anchored out in the middle of the bay and there's water all around. Usually get a chance to go ashore 2 or 3 times a week though when in port and our section doesn't have the duty. Sometimes get the weekend off, Saturday & Sunday.

I've been going ashore quite a bit lately. Rated liberty Memorial Day so went over to 'Diego and watched the parade. Really had a nice long parade, Army, Navy, Marines, American Legion and a lot of other stuff.

Last Saturday night I went roller skating. Sun. afternoon I went to Balboa Park. This is a large park just outside of 'Diego. Covers hundreds of acres. They also have museums and a zoo there. Costs two bits to get into the zoo and another quarter bus fare for a three mile ride and a lecture on different animals. They sure have a lot of them there. Every animal you could think of is there. Even elephants, giraffes, hippopotamus. Feels good to get off the ship once in a while and get some good solid ground and green grass under my feet.

Suppose everything is pretty nice back home about this time of the year too. Going to seem kind of funny not to be working at the factory this summer, but I'm glad I don't have to work there this year. Wonder how much they're paying this season after that wage & hour law went into effect?

What's John doing now, working for the silo company? You didn't tell me in your last letter. Is Karl down at Waterville steady? How's he getting along with the v-8? Suppose Pa is still driving the Chevy.

Well, tomorrow John will be 18 yrs old. Give him my best wishes. Tell him to drop me a line sometime and let me know how he's making out, and how everything is with the old gang from St. Peter. It gets kind of lonesome at times even if a fellow has got a lot of pals aboard ship. Still they aren't the same old friends I know back home.

Having pretty nice weather here, but it's always damp being on the ocean this way. The days are cool and the nights are almost too cool. In the evening when we watch the movie on the top side we wear sweaters and pea coats. You remember that p-coat I wore home on leave don't you. At night a guy has to use two blankets to keep from getting cold.

Get a lot better show aboard ship than at the training station.

I get the Le Sueur Herald once a week so find out pretty much of what's going on back there.

Broke my wrist watch while standing a starboard look-out watch one night on the way back from Equador. Cost me $3.25 to have it fixed again.

I'm sitting in the mess hall writing this letter. It's about time for the movie to start so guess I'll go up on the main deck and watch it. We have a show aboard ship every evening when the weather permits. Doesn't cost us anything to see it, of course. Also have radio in the compartments below and a fellow comes aboard and sells papers every morning whenever we're in port, so keep in touch with the outside world that way.

Suppose you read about the submarine that sunk in the Atlantic a couple weeks ago and 26 sailors lost their lives. All the boys here felt pretty bad about it.

Will have to sign off now. Best wishes to everyone at home. Drop a line soon. I always look forward to getting a letter. Won't be long now until Katrina is a year old. Hardly seems that long ago since she was born.

Well good bye and good luck. I'll be looking for a letter soon. Same address.

Your son, Bill

***

U. S. S. Preston – 379
San Diego, Calif
Sunday, June 25, 1939
Dear Mother,

Your letter came a few days ago. I have plenty time on my hands this forenoon, so will try to write a few lines. I'm feeling top notch as always. Had a tooth filled a couple days ago. I weighed myself yesterday. I weigh 187 lbs believe it or not. Maybe a few days of real hard work on a farm would take a few pounds off me. There isn't much hard work aboard ship but it gets pretty tiresome anyhow doing the same thing every day. Sweeping and swabbing decks, shinning brass, chipping paint and painting. Then there's always a boatswains-mate standing over a fellow telling him just how to do the work. On a farm a fellow has a chance to figure out a few things for himself, but here they think for you.

Had the destroyer in floating dry-dock three days last week. Just got out of there yesterday. We scraped and painted her hull and bottom. Kept us busy for a while getting the scales and barnacles off her. She looked pretty nice after the job was done. A ship sure looks big when it's out of the water. Makes a fellow feel pretty small when he stands underneath it and looks up.

We're still stationed at 'Diego. Have only been on two cruises since we came back. One for three days and the other lasted four days. On these cruises we go out on the ocean and have depth sounding, direction finding, gun training and torpedo school.

Have been out to Mission Beach twice swimming in the ocean. I was out there yesterday. It's about 4 miles out of San Diego. Costs 25 cents out there on streetcar and 35 cents for use of the bath house lockers.

This California is a high priced place. They charge two prices for everything. Thirty-six dollars a month doesn't go very far here. I thought when I got in the navy I'd be able to save a few dollars, but just seems impossible. Costs 15 cents to take a shore boat just to get away from the ship and the same to get back. Or a fellow can go on the ship's boats free then take a streetcar from 28ᵗʰ street but it amounts to about the same.

On a weekend liberty over Saturday and Sunday a fellow has to rent a room and buy his meals if he goes ashore. Costs 50 cents for a good meal. A guy just has to go ashore whenever he gets a chance. Staying aboard ship is just like being in a house all the time. We have a lot of fun though just the same. Most of the boys are young like myself. Good fellows most of them.

They have a free movie aboard ship every night. So we get to see plenty shows.

The weather doesn't change much around here. It never gets hot here on the ocean and the nights are damp and cool. Sure a lot different from Minnesota.

Glad to hear that everything is O.K. back home. Wish you would write more often though. I always wonder how everything is back east.

I figure on going to the air show at Linda Vista north of San Diego this afternoon so guess I'll have to close for this time and get into my dress blues and get my liberty card.

Give my greetings to all the family.

Your loving son, Bill

***

During the summer months of 1939, Karin struggled more than ever with her "sad time." Jana did all that she could to help at home, even to the point of taking over writing letters to Bill. She would be twelve years old in August but found herself pretty much in charge of running the household. She felt that somebody needed to keep in touch with Bill as his letters home reflected some lonesome times that he talked about when he thought about being so far from home. So Jana did the best she could and kept writing while Karin was unable to do so.

***

U.S.S. Preston
San Diego, Calif.
Sun. July 30, 1939
Dear Sis (Jana),

Thanks for the letter I received from you the other day. It helps a lot to hear from home when a fella is so far away from everyone he knows.

Most people think of a sailor as a carefree, happy-go-lucky chap who hasn't anything much to do but enjoy himself. That's a long ways from the truth because even life aboard ship can get very tiresome and dull. Same old routine day after day with nothing much of news to write about.

Sometimes we go to sea and stay out on maneuvers for a whole week, other times we go out each morning and come back home to port at sunset each day. Then too at times we just lay at anchor in the harbor for several days.

A guy can't write much about the ocean. One square mile of water looks pretty much like another. Nothing but water and more water for a whole week wherever you look.

Usually when I go ashore I go up to the park for a while where I can see the trees and feel the soft grass under my feet instead of a steel deck all the time. A person doesn't appreciate things of that sort until you get away from it.

I go ashore about once or twice a week when we happen to be in port and I rate liberty.

Well, I'm still slinging hash in other words, mess cooking yet. Have been at this job for a month now. Have two more months of it yet till I get back on the deck force. I don't mind it though. I get about $10.00 a month extra. Of course I have to work every day. These gobs got a habit of wanting 3 squares a day.

Last week we were out at sea having torpedo school shooting torpedoes. When the torpedoes are fired they travel under water and when they run out of power they come to the surface and float. Then we steam over there and hoist them aboard to be used again. They can travel from 3-6 miles. There were two seaplanes with our division last week. The pilots can see where the torpedoes are and signal to the ship. These torpedoes cost several thousand dollars each so it's quite an expense if they lose any.

There are four destroyers in our division the *Perkins, Cushing, Smith* and *Preston.* All ships in the navy are painted light gray. Last Friday our division was camouflaged. They painted the ships dark green and dark gray. They sure look different now. They camouflage the ships so it will be harder for the enemy to see us. Tomorrow we go out again for more torpedo school. Hope the ocean doesn't get too rough. I've only been seasick once so far and hope I don't ever get it again.

The weather stays quite a bit the same here on the sea. It isn't any warmer or cooler now than it was in May when I first came here.

Well kid, it's soon your birthday again. I'll try to find some nice souvenir in Diego to send to you.

Got a letter from Anna a couple days ago so guess I'll have to end this letter so I can write a few lines to her too.

What's John doing now? Suppose he will be working in the factory again in corn pack.

Hope this finds everybody at home feeling well. I'm O.K.

I bought a uniform of tailor made blues for $28.00. It looks pretty nice.

I get the Le Sueur Herald every Monday morning so I keep up with what's going on back there. They sure give that swimming pool a big play up.

I'd like to write to Lorraine too but it's pretty hard to write to everyone. Give her my regards.

Tell John to throw some ink this way soon when he isn't too busy pitching bundles.

I might get a few days leave this fall so I can come home if I can ever save up $100 for train fare. At least I'll be seeing you in a year or two.

Write again soon. Best wishes to all the family.

Sincerely, Your Brother Bill

***

When Bill was changed from the deck gang to galley duty, his first response was disappointment. He so wanted to be a part of the "black-gang", the engineers on the ship. They were really important in his eyes because it was up to them to keep the ship going. This was where you really could advance in your rating and the boost in pay would be nice also.

But he made the best of the situation and soon adapted to his rotation in "mess cooking". He knew his way around a stove thanks to what he had learned in his experiences in CCC Camp cooking and his time spent in the galley while in boot camp. The biggest difference was trying to cook a meal while keeping the pots and pans on the stove when the ship was out of port and the Preston hit rough seas. That was a challenge. And it seemed that no sooner were the last of the dishes scrubbed from breakfast, and it was time to get the noon meal going.

He soon became friends with another young sailor who was also taking his galley rotation. Jim Spillman was from rural Mississippi and both young men made it a practice to spend time together when their shift was complete. They often went topside on the deck to have a cigarette before heading to their bunks to catch some much needed sleep. They found it easy to talk to each other and everything from tough days working on the farm to the beautiful girls back home was covered.

One day Jim excitedly took a letter from his pocket to share with Bill. "Look-a- here Bill," he exclaimed in his slow, southern drawl. "I got this picture from Gladys, my girlfriend. Ain't she a beauty?" he went on. Bill took the picture from him to see a beautiful, dark-haired young girl with a smile that would melt anyone's heart. "Well, you sure know how to pick 'em," Bill replied at the same time wishing that he could share a picture also. The closest he had to any kind of girlfriend was his recent meeting of Paula Manley. And this was just the very beginning of a friendship, nothing more, yet Bill found himself thinking of her often and hoping that her promise to write would materialize.

In early August of 1939, Bill did finally get a letter from Paula with fantastic news. She was coming to California and going to look for work there. As soon as he read her letter, he immediately wrote back and plans were made to meet when she arrived in San Diego. He was so anxious to see her again but in the meantime, life in the Navy went on.

The Preston continued maneuvers at sea and short range battle practice was a part of that. Bill and the other men were amazed at the loudness of the big guns on the ship when they were fired during this practice. All were ordered to put cotton in their ears to prevent their ear drums from rupturing but this did little to muffle the loud sound of the guns. The whole ship pitched from the vibrations and it was hard to keep steady footing no matter where one was on the ship.

After getting back into port in September, the Preston was positioned alongside the tender Whitney, and was to undergo a three week overhaul. Bill was happy to get liberty his first weekend back and as soon as he gathered his gear, he headed ashore. Banks of lockers were available to rent nearby. Bill had rented a locker on his first stop in San Diego and had some civilian clothes stored there. He was proud to wear his Navy uniform, but now and then it felt good to look like a civilian again.

As soon as he got changed and found a bus, he headed to the street where Paula had rented a room. He was not sure that she would be at home, but he took the chance that she would be and he was really excited about seeing her again. By the time he reached her address, it was around eight o'clock in the evening. He found the boarding house, entered the front room and inquired about Paula. He was directed to a room upstairs, down the hallway, third door on the left. He took the steps, two at a time, and knocked on the door of her room.

Paula was there and opened the door, surprised to see Bill standing there. "Well, hello there, Bill," she exclaimed excitedly. "I'm sure glad to see you again." Bill was not certain if he should shake hands; give her a hug or what. "Well, the same goes here," he offered. "How are you doing with the job?" he questioned. "Oh for goodness sakes," she replied. "Let's not stand here in the hall. Come on in and sit down."

After exchanging news of what each had been doing, they left the boarding house and walked down the street to a small café on the corner. Paula told Bill that she had eaten supper there several times and that the cook made really good pies. They walked to the café only to find it already closed for the evening. They opted to sit on the bus stop bench to continue their conversation.

After what seemed like just a few minutes, Paula glanced at her watch to see that it was nearly midnight. It was time for her to return to her room as she had to be at work by 8:00 the next morning and it was a twenty minute bus ride to the office. Slowly they walked back to the boarding house, hand in hand. Neither of them thought about taking the other's hand, it just kind of happened.

Once back at the boarding house, Bill leaned over to kiss Paula on her forehead. "Oh come on, you can do better than that," Paula teased. So he did and each immediately understood that this new friendship was going to be something special! Plans were made for them to meet on Sunday when Bill would have liberty again. Paula suggested they go to church together, and then have Sunday dinner at the little café.

In Bill's next letter to Jana he wrote, "It gets kind of lonesome for home here at times but I don't seem to mind it so much now since Paula came here." Bill and Paula continued to see each other each time that Bill got liberty. Then on October 5th, the Preston left San Diego for Pearl Harbor, Hawaii. Bill wondered if Paula would be content to only be able to see him occasionally when he was in port. Some of his shipmates had warned him that girlfriends are gone about the same time as the ship weighs anchor. And in some sad cases, the same was true of wives!

***

Pearl Harbor, Honolulu
T.H.
October 15, 1939
Dear Mom,

At last I'm out at the place where the rainbow ends, where the grass is always green & it never snows. On the Island of Oahu, paradise of the Pacific more commonly known as "the rock" among sailors.

We left San Diego, Thursday the 5th of Oct. A lot of ships came down here. There must be over 10,000 sailors in our detachment. Took us a week to come down, arrived last Thurs. 12th. It's about 2, 200 miles from here to California, but we traveled nearly 3,000 miles doing a lot of zig-zagging around on fleet tactics.

We are laying at anchor in Pearl Harbor now. The nearest city is Honolulu, it's 7 miles from here. Costs $.50 round trip there by taxi. I've only made one liberty there so far. That was last Friday. Another fellow & I went ashore together. I got a hair cut first of all. They have Japanese & Hawaiian girls as barbers here. First time I ever had a lady barber give me a haircut.

Then we went out to the beach at Waikiki and swam all afternoon. Certainly is nice, the sandy beach and warm ocean water. I rented a pair of trunks & a towel.

There are a lot of coconut palms there so we got hungry for coconuts. I just had my trunks on. I climbed up a tree about 30 ft. high and picked a couple ripe ones. Didn't have much trouble getting up but skinned my shins getting down again. Those nuts sure were good, cool milk in them too. Took about an hour to peel the husk off and break them open. Had more fun than a bushel of monkeys. Later we went to a dance at the Y.M.C.A.

Then back to the ship again. Liberty is up at 11:00 P.M. each night. Back in the States we could stay out all night till 7:30 the next morning.

Yesterday & today I went swimming in the pool at the submarine base. Guess I'll go to Honolulu tomorrow evening and mail this letter.

These Hawaiian girls certainly are good looking, even prettier than I thought they would be. Get a lot of Hawaiian guitar music on the radio and some of their speaking, but most of the people speak English, nice people, so courteous and hospitable.

The rainy season is just starting now. It rains every day, it's a warm rain and the sun comes out every few minutes between showers. Gets almost too hot for comfort at times. You can see a rainbow nearly every hour of the day. Lot of green sugar cane & pineapple fields & palm trees. They should have named this island Emerald Isle instead of Oahu. It's about 140 miles around the whole island. There are several islands in this group, this is one of the largest. Mountains & hills in the center.

Haven't heard from Paula yet but expect a letter any day. Said she was going up to Los Angeles to visit her aunt while I was gone. Hope I don't get permanent duty at Honolulu even though I like it. Give my best regards to all of the family. Write soon, you can send a letter to me at the usual 3 cents postage. Well, Mom I've been on the east coast to the west, to South America and Honolulu and still haven't found the golden shoe to send to you but I'll keep on looking for it.

Your loving son, Bill

***

U. S. Naval Hospital
October 29, 1939
Pearl Harbor, T.H.
Dear Mother,
Your letter came yesterday. I guess I never was so glad to get a letter before. As you see by the heading I'm in the hospital again. Appendicitis this time.

On Friday, the 20th of October, I woke up about 2:00 A.M. with awful pains in my stomach. Kept getting worse & worse. Finally at 6:00 A.M. they put me in a stretcher and in a boat & took me ashore. Called an ambulance, which brought me to the hospital. Lucky that we were in port at the time, as there is no doctor on our ship, just a pharmacist's mate 1st class.

Didn't take ether or a shot in the spine, just gave me a couple shots with a needle full of something or other right around the place where he was going to perform the operation. Hurt like the very devil when he started operating. I guess I was as white around the gills as the time I had my tonsils taken out. Put in 7 steel clips in the incision.

The first four days I didn't get a thing to eat. Practically lived on black coffee, cigarettes & morphine. Got pretty tiresome just lying in bed. Tues. the doc took the clips out. Wed morning I got up and walked around some. There were about 50 other guys in the same ward. Changed me to an outside bunk in a screened in wing. It's fairly cool out here but gets pretty hot at times.

This is a big hospital, hundreds of fellows here suffering from everything from growing pains to approaching old age. So I have lots of company.

Have been up every day since last Wed. doing light work like sweeping, etc.

Been here 9 days now, guess I'll be here another week or two yet. I feel fine though so don't worry. Eat like a horse. Boy we sure get good food here. Best eats I've had anywhere. Really isn't such a bad vacation after all, but gets pretty tiresome being in one place so long.

Everything is nice & green outside. Flowers blooming. Lot of rain now during the rainy season. It rained six inches last Sun. P.M. to evening.

Had a little bad luck aboard ship before I left. The day after payday somebody got in my locker & stole $5.00 from me, the money I had left from that payday. Oh well, glad it wasn't more.

There's 4 ½ hrs. difference in time between here & Minn. When it's 12:00 o'clock noon here, it's 4:30 P.M. back there.

I just came out of the dressing room now. The doctor lanced the wound so it would drain better. Write soon & send the letter to the same address that you have. I'll be back on ship by the time it gets here. So long or as the Hawaiians say "Aloha". Best wishes to all.

Your son, Bill

***

Bill was back aboard ship, all recovered from the appendectomy when a letter came from Karl telling him that Karin had been hospitalized for depression. Jana, Lorraine and Katrina had been staying with George and Selma Anderley. Lars worked with George and when Karin had to go to the hospital, Lars just didn't know what he was going to do for someone to care for his girls. George said that they could stay with he and Selma until Karin was able to come home again. It seemed a reasonable arrangement but after one week, the older girls wanted to go back home. Jana reasoned that she could manage to care for herself and Lorraine, and it was a shorter walk to school for them too. So they moved home once again. It was decided that Katrina would remain with the Anderleys since she was less than two years old. Jana and Lorraine managed to get themselves off to school each day and Lars kept working in order to provide for his family.

This news from home was a worry for Bill, but as it was, there was nothing that he could do to help.

***

Pearl Harbor, T. H.
Dec. 27, 1939
Hello Karl,
Received your letter some time ago so will scratch a few lines and try to get it in the mail. The mail ship leaves tomorrow for the mainland.

Sorry to hear that mother is sick and I wish there was something I could do. Would like to get a month's leave and go home but that's next to impossible.

Well, Xmas came and went. Wasn't any different from any other day in the navy. Had a good dinner though Xmas day. Then in the afternoon I went swimming. Go sun bathing and swimming nearly every time that I rate liberty in the afternoon or weekend.

We leave here the 5th of January, so should get to Mare Island, 'Frisco about the 12th of next month.

Really haven't much to say. Nothing unusual has happened since I wrote last. We haven't been to sea at all this month so it's been a little easier than during maneuvers.

We'll be in dry-dock at Mare Island for 2 or 3 months. That's where the work really is. Everything has to be repaired or replaced. The entire ship has to be scraped & repainted from stem to stern.

I think we will go back out here for permanent duty after the overhaul and fleet problem is over. I'd rather be stationed in the states but then a fellow can't pick the port he wishes, just have to go where we are sent.

I'm going to try to get 7 days leave when we get back to the states so I can go see Paula. She's working at Escondido, California now. That's about 500 miles south of 'Frisco. I'll just about be able to make it down there, have a short visit and get back home to the Preston again in a week.

I had liberty this afternoon so went over to the yard "Y" and am writing this letter from there.

We're wearing white uniforms now since we came down here. The weather doesn't change much. About 70' or 80' above. The grass and trees are green and the flowers blooming, so it's pretty nice as far as environment goes.

Hope Mom is better by now. Best wishes to the family. Drop a line soon again. The next time you write, address your letter to: S. S. S. Preston, Mare Island, California c/o postmaster. I'll be looking for a letter when I get back.

Good Luck. As Ever, Bill

***

Regardless of the fact that Hawaii was a scenic paradise and the tropical days so warm and pleasant, it was a relief for Bill to go back to the mainland once again.

In a letter to Karl, Bill described leaving Hawaii. *"The parting wasn't quite like the movies would picture it. No fond Aloha's sung by some dusky maiden or leis tossed tenderly from the dock. When the navy leaves port, they just weigh the mud-hook, hoist the speed-cones and steam for other parts. So we cast off the howsers and pointed her bow in the direction of 'Frisco. The crossing was uneventful, lot of rough weather and cold sea watching. She pitched and rolled the entire distance of 2,100 miles."*

The Preston arrived in California on January 11, 1940. As they neared San Francisco, Bill was excited to see the landmarks of this city as they sailed into port. He marveled at the size and scope of the Golden Gate Bridge as they passed under that. His eyes turned towards the grim looking Alcatraz and the sign painted nearby, "Warning, Alcatraz. Keep Away." Bill thought to himself that warning might be taken in several ways!

As they continued towards port, Bill could see the Oakland Bay Bridge and Treasure Island. Their final destination was Mare Island Naval Yards near the city of Vallejo, where their ship was scheduled for a complete overhaul. He was looking forward to a change of scene and also held on to the hope that he would get leave in March and be able to go see Paula in Escondido. They had kept in touch by letters while he was gone and this only increased his desire to see her again in person. He hoped that he would not be assigned to permanent duty in Hawaii, nice as that was. It was just too far away from Paula.

He wondered where the Preston would be ordered to next, once they left dry-dock. Would it be Pearl Harbor, San Diego or maybe China?

Bill was also looking forward to drawing more pay as a Seaman 1ˢᵗ Class. He had recently taken the written exams for this and felt confident that he would be rated after all the hard work he had put into studying for the test. It would really be good to get a raise to $54 a month, up from his current pay of $36 a month.

Near the end of February, Bill was able to get liberty and made a bus trip to San Diego to see Paula. The trip was nearly 500 miles and he only had two and a half days liberty, so the visit was short. But it was so good to see Paula again and they managed to enjoy their time together, limited as it was. They were able to see several movies, one of which was "The Grapes of Wrath, starring Henry Fonda. They also went to see Chinatown one evening. It was quite an experience to see so many Oriental people and all the shop signs written in Chinese. Neither Bill nor Paula could understand or question why so many people chose to live and work in one area, much less imagine the fear that existed among the Chinese if they ventured beyond certain perimeters.

Once back on Mare Island, the work on the complete overhaul of the Preston continued. After all the engines were put back on the ship, it was completely repainted. Then it was time to reload with ammunition; torpedoes, warheads, depth charges and small arms ammunition. The twenty- five pound shells for the five inch guns seemed to weigh a ton each after they were carried by the men up several flights of ladders from the fantail to the forecastle deck at the bow of the ship. Everyone was glad when this job was completed. The Preston was once again underway after her overhaul by mid-March and soon was back in San Diego. After just a few days there, she once again returned to San Francisco to rejoin the rest of the fleet. Then it was off to Pearl Harbor, Hawaii for six weeks of maneuvers.

During these maneuvers the fleet simulated actual war-fare as closely as possible.

In his next letter to Karin, Bill shared some exciting news.

"Well, after months of trying, I finally got out of the deck force and into the engineer's force. More commonly known as the "black-gang" because it's so greasy and dirty around the boilers and turbines where we work. I'm a "snipe" now. That's the nickname for all firemen…. My rate is Fireman Second Class.…It sure is hot working in the fire-room keeping the boilers fired. It's 106˚ temperature down there now while we're in port and it gets a lot hotter when we have all the burners lit off while at sea. A fellow sweats from the minute he goes down there till he is relieved by the next watch. This steam business is pretty complicated to me yet, but if I study and work hard I should be able to get the hang of it after a while".

What he didn't share with his mother was some bad news that he had gotten from Paula shortly after he returned to Mare Island. She wrote saying that as much as she thought of him, their long distance relationship was just not something that she wanted to continue. It was especially hard for her when she learned that he was going back to Hawaii once again. Paula was ready to settle down in one place, get married and raise a family. She couldn't see how staying with Bill was going to work because of all the time they would be separated while he was in the Navy, and so she thought it best to break things off now before they got more serious about each other.

At first he was devastated. He truly cared for Paula and thought they might eventually build a life together. Once the shock wore off, he became angry for a while, then as the weeks went by, and he got accustomed to his new duties in the "black-gang" he began to find a sense of relief in working as hard as he did. He thought seriously about putting in a request for Asiatic duty when three shipmates were sent to China. It would really be fascinating to see that part of the world. And why not if you were not encumbered by a wife and family.

Since his immediate circumstances now did not include a girl-friend, his thoughts turned toward home again and his letters inquired about his family so far away in Minnesota.

"Soon it will be summer again back home. Out here you can't hardly tell the difference. Only that it gets a little cooler and we have more rain in the winter than in the summer...........Karl seems to be making out O.K. with his truck. I wish him all the luck in the world..................Anna has her hands full with the babies to take care of.........I'd sure like to see that little squirt, Katrina now. Wonder if she would dislike me as much as she did last year. Remember how she would holler when I picked her up?"

When the maneuvers out of Pearl Harbor were over, Bill was able to enjoy a liberty at Lahina on the island of Maui. He was one of nearly 30,000 sailors on liberty at the same time after eleven days at sea. Getting back on board ship took nearly three hours because the liberty boats transporting men back to their ships were overwhelmed with so many sailors to haul. Once back on board, the next sail was 1000 miles north of Hawaii, nearly halfway to Alaska. Then it was back to Pearl Harbor and a much more relaxing time in port because the "war games" were over and it was not necessary to "darken ship and man battle stations" every night.

The "war games" aka maneuvers involving the Navy were a very necessary part of preparing the United States for possible involve-ment in another war. Europe was continuing to struggle under the advance of Nazism and Japan emulated the German pattern by their growing invasions in Asia.

Because of racial and cultural differences, the relationships between Japan and the western world were strained. Neither group of people understood or trusted the other. In 1923 Japan's eco-nomic situation worsened because of a huge earthquake. A world-wide depression intensified this crisis. The League of Nations had been established following World War I as a means to promote and insure world peace. Japan remained a part of the League until the Chinese threatened their position in Manchuria and Japan resigned their League membership in 1933. By 1940 Japan invaded French Indo China(Viet-Nam) and then went on to join the axis powers of Germany and Italy. This alliance was on their way to world domination and appeared as a major threat to other peaceful countries. The United States and Great Britain reacted with an oil boycott against Japan. This prompted Japan to invade oil-rich Indonesia and consider a war with the United States and Great Britain. At the peak of Japanese power, they controlled all lands from Japan to the border of India in the west and south to New Guinea.

The plans for the Preston to return again to San Diego from Hawaii were thwarted by accelerating war conditions in the world. Germany undertook further domination of Europe by an invasion of Holland and the United States was alerted to the possibility that Japan would try to grab the oil rich lands in Dutch East Indies while Holland was occupied defending their homeland and unable to defend their colonies in the East Indies.

So the Navy remained in Hawaii in the outside chance anything like this would happen and they might be ordered into war. The Preston remained anchored near Maui while various tactics were practiced: submarine sounding and anti-aircraft gun practice. Most of the weeks between May and July 1940 were spent at sea in these various tactics. Then Bill wrote home to say that he was back in Pearl Harbor again and would be there for about three weeks. His duty had been changed again, back to mess cooking for the next three months. He voiced his wish that this would be his last rotation through the kitchen! On a positive note, he shared the news that he was happy that he passed the exam for Fireman 1st Class and that he was certain to be rated as such very soon.

***

U. S. S. Preston
Pearl Harbor T.H.
August 25, 1940
My dear Mother,

I received your letter today. I was very happy to hear from you but it made me so sad to find out that you were in the State Hospital. Of course Anna and Jana have been writing to me this summer and told me you were in the hospital but they never mentioned what one.

I wrote to you several times last spring but never got an answer. I thought maybe you didn't get my letter was the reason that you didn't write. I'm ashamed of myself that I didn't keep writing. Please forgive me for being so careless. But don' think that I forget you, Mother. I've thought of you every day since I left home last year. I wanted to get leave so I could go home to visit everyone again but I've been out here in Hawaii most of the time. And of course it's impossible to get leave and go way back there. It's over 4,000 miles you know.

However we got some good news the other day. The whole fleet that is out here is supposed to go back to San Diego, California for two weeks. A few ships at a time. From what I hear the Preston is supposed to leave here the 23rd of September and arrive in San Diego the 1st of Oct. Stay in San Diego for 2 weeks and then go back to Hawaii.

And every man on the ship is supposed to get 5 days leave. Of course I wouldn't be able to go to Minnesota and back to California in such a short time but I'm going to try to get a longer leave. Emergency leave it's called. I'll talk to my division officer and have him explain to the captain how it is. And if it's possible I think he will let me go for that time. I don't know if it will work but I sincerely hope so.

I want to see you as much as you want to see me.

Yesterday was Jana's birthday. I sent her a kimono and a coconut hand carved belt a couple weeks ago for a present. I think she's got it by now. I hope she likes it.

Just think she's thirteen years old now. It seems like an awful long time ago since she was born doesn't it? Still I can remember it as if it were yesterday. The next morning when Dad and Karl came home and got John and I we went out to New Ulm in the old Model T Ford to see you. And John and I were so happy to have a baby sister.

I don't hear from John or Karl anymore. It's been over a half a year ago now since either one of them wrote to me. I guess they intend to, but just keep putting it off. Jana and Anna write though and I'm glad they don't forget.

I'm mess cooking again on the ship. I started the 1ˢᵗ of July and I keep on until the 1ˢᵗ of Oct. then I go back to the fire-room and work. I haven't been off the ship for 25 days now so haven't been anywhere lately. Not much to write about what we're doing out here. Just the same old thing, maneuvering around most of the summer. And then in port part of the time.

We were over to Hilo for the fourth of July. That's a city on another island. It's about 150 miles from here. I went ashore a couple times. It's real nice there. And I enjoyed it a lot.

I must stop writing now but I will write again soon, I promise. I hope you get better soon, Mother dear. I'll try very hard to get leave so I can come and see you in Oct. I hope I can if nothing goes wrong so they change the orders and keep us out here.

Goodbye for this time and may God keep you safe for me.

Your loving son, Bill

***

True to his word, Bill did talk to his division officer explaining the situation with Karin's hospitalization. He was granted an emergency leave and as soon as the Preston docked in San Diego, Bill headed to the train station to get on the next available train that would take him to Minnesota. The long ride to Mankato seemed as lengthy as the last months at sea. He was so anxious to get back home and see his family again and especially to see Karin for himself and find out how ill she was and if she was making any recovery from the depression that had taken her to such depths. John was at the depot when train #58 arrived around seven o'clock in the evening. He anxiously searched the crowd of passengers departing the train until at last he spotted his brother dressed in Navy blues.

"Bill, Bill," John shouted. "I'm over here." Bill had been looking around the station and didn't see John right away, but as soon as he did he bounded over to him and went from a handshake to a brotherly embrace in a moment. "How're you doing, kid?" he asked. Soon the brothers, plus Bill's gear, were in the car, heading down the road to Le Sueur. Along the way, Bill threw the questions to his brother about everyone and how they were, what they were doing. Most all of the questions were about Karin. Bill was anxious to stop by the hospital to see his mother, but John informed him that visiting hours were over for that day and that he could come back tomorrow in the afternoon to see their mother.

As they neared St. Peter, John suggested that they stop for a hamburger and a beer. John turned the car into the parking lot at Hank's Place before Bill could answer, yes or no. Soon they were seated in a booth and a pretty blond waitress approached the booth to take their order.

"Hi, Annette," John said. "How's it going? This swabbie is my ugly brother Bill." Annette quickly answered, "I don't think he's ugly at all. Downright handsome in his Navy blues." As soon as Annette left to place their order at the kitchen window, Bill turned to his brother to say, "Where has this beauty been all my life?" John proceeded to inform him that she was originally from Le Sueur, graduated from high school last year and was working to make some money so that she could go on to teachers college later. In a short time their beer was served and soon Annette returned with their hamburger orders.

As the brothers finished their meal and continued the drive to Le Sueur Bill commented that he couldn't tell if that was the best or worst hamburger he'd ever had. He was much more interested in this waitress!!

The rest of the drive to Le Sueur went by quickly and soon they were crossing the bridge into town and heading up the hill to Third Street and the rental house that was home for the Persson family. Bill wondered if his younger sisters would be awake to greet him as it was now nine o'clock on a school night. He opened the back door to see Jana sitting at the kitchen table, pencil in hand, struggling with the mysteries of 8th grade history class. As soon as she heard the door open and saw Bill standing there, she jumped up from the chair and ran to hug her brother.

"Whoa there, little Sis," Bill teased, "Save some of those hugs for a while. I'll be home for a week you know." He crossed the kitchen and entered the front room. Lars was dozing in the rocking chair and Lorraine was curled up on a day bed, fast asleep. Lars awoke to the sound of footsteps and quickly stood up to embrace Bill. "Oh, son," he began. "You just can't know how glad I am to see you again. We have missed you so much and now with your mother so ill.........." The words tightened in his throat and his eyes misted over. "I know, Dad, I know," Bill offered in comfort.

John came into the room, said a few words to Lars, and then announced that he had to drive back to Cleveland because his employer, Mr. Wolf was going to start picking corn in the morning and he needed John to help. John said that he would be back on Saturday evening and he and Bill could see what was going on then. Maybe they'd go to a dance in Mankato or something. Bill agreed, and after sharing good-byes, he left and the rest of the Persson family continued chatting for a while. Then it was time for the girls to go to bed as the next day was Friday and they had to go to school.

Bill picked the sleeping Lorraine up from the day bed and carried her upstairs to the bedroom that she and Jana shared. Once downstairs again, he heard Lars locking the kitchen door and turning off the light. The two continued talking for a while and plans were set for Bill to drive Lars to work in the morning so that he could use the car to go to St. Peter to visit Karin. It had been a long, long train riding day for Bill and he was happy when Lars announced that it was bedtime for them too.

Bill climbed back upstairs and crawled into the metal frame bed that he and John had shared for years. The next thing he knew, he heard the sounds of his sisters getting up to get ready for school. Then the welcoming smell of perking coffee brought him to the day. What a short night that was!

Lars was pouring cereal into bowls for the girls' breakfasts when Bill walked into the kitchen. "I smelled the coffee and here I am," he went on. "Hey there, short stuff," he said to Lorraine, "do you remember who carried you to bed last night?" Shyly Lorraine looked at her brother and said, "I thought it was a handsome prince." Bill chuckled to himself as he poured a cup of coffee. "Well it's a good thing it was a handsome prince and not some ugly stranger!!" Soon the girls finished their breakfast and gathered up coats and books on their way out the door to school.

Shortly after the girls left, it was time to take Lars to work also. Bill returned to take a bath and shave before getting on with the day. It seemed so unusual to be alone in this house. His memories were of happier days when Karin's presence made a home. He thought back to his leave after boot camp. Karin had made one of his favorite meals, though at the time she was not completely well. After eating, he had gotten up from his chair, gave his mother a hug and thanked her for the delicious food. She just smiled up at him and said, "that's what mothers do, son, take care of their children." But now she couldn't do this and he thought about his younger sisters and what they had been missing. He had been gone for well over a year now so maybe things had been different for a long time, even before Karin went to the hospital. There was also the issue of his mother being in a State Mental Hospital and the perceived shame to that. It was one thing to be in the hospital for appendicitis but quite another to be there for treatment of mental problems!

He learned the news about Karin's hospitalization in letters from his sisters but they neglected to tell him where she had been sent. Karin's depression had been in evidence for years, primarily flaring after the birth of a baby. But this past year the episodes were longer, resulting in hospitalization for treatment. He was really anxious to see her for himself and get a good idea of just how she was doing and what kind of treatment she was undergoing.

Once cleaned up and dressed for the day in his blue uniform, he headed out the door again, this time turning down Fourth Street towards Anna and Mel's apartment. He was anxious to see his older sister again; her letters to him were always a welcome part of mail call. He loved hearing about her little ones, he appreciated her efforts to write because he knew that it took a great deal of time to care for a two year old girl and a boy of ten months.

The sun was bright against the blue October sky and it truly was a beautiful fall day in Minnesota. The mild autumn weather gave one final touch of brilliant color to the leaves that still clung to the trees. Bill hummed to himself as he jumped out of the car, then ran up the stairs to the second floor apartment.

He raised his hand to knock at the door, listening to the sounds coming from inside. The children were crying and sounds from the baby grew louder as Anna came to answer the door. She opened the door to a wonderful surprise. There stood Bill with his big smile that she had missed seeing for much too long.

"Oh, Bill, come in," Anna said. "I'm sorry it's so messy and noisy in here. Little Ann has a tummy ache and the baby is teething."

"I'm here to give you a hand, ma'am," Bill answered. "Let's see if we can get at least one of these youngsters happy again." He bent over and swooped up Little Ann before she had a chance to react and being surprised in this manner quickly shut off her tears. Bill carried the little girl across the room and to the sofa where a small Teddy Bear was tossed onto a cushion.

"Who is this guy?" Bill questioned his niece. "Lonzo," she answered quickly in her limited two year old language. Soon she was laughing as Bill bounced Lonzo up the "mountain" on the back of the sofa, then slid the bear downwards into the "ocean." Baby Eddie temporarily forgot his teething discomfort as he watched the antics from the safety of his mother's arms.

"Oh Bill, Anna exclaimed. "You are just what I needed this morning. A helping hand!" Bill handed Lonzo to his niece and she began to play the same game that Bill had started. Anna sat Eddie down on the floor in front of the sofa and handed him another stuffed toy. Soon his "horsie" was running along the sofa and falling into the "ocean" too.

Bill and Anna found chairs in the kitchen while the children were amusing themselves and conversation turned to news about everyone in the family. Anna related that Jana and Lorraine seemed to be doing all right by staying at home with Lars, but that she had not heard anything about Katrina for some time. Bill said that he hoped it would be all right with Mrs. Anderley if he came to see little Katrina while he was home on leave. Anna was certain that Selma would be glad to have him come by for a visit.

Anna glanced at the clock on the kitchen wall, and saw that it was after eleven and soon lunchtime for the children. She got up from her chair and went to the small refrigerator across the room. "Would you like to stay for lunch with us, Bill," she inquired of her brother. "I'll stay as long as I'm welcome," he answered. "Good! That's settled. I'll heat up the last of my homemade potato soup and we'll have jelly-bread to go with it. The kids like this," Ann stated.

"That sounds really good, Sis," Bill answered. "There's nothing like a warm bowl of soup in October to make you feel all warm and ready for the world," he continued.

Lunch passed quickly and once the last of the bowls and plates were washed and put away, it was time to get Little Ann and Eddie down for afternoon naps. After good-bye hugs to all, Bill left the apartment, then headed out the door with a promise to see them again before his leave was over.

He decided to take the gravel road through the sleepy little town of Ottawa on the way to St. Peter. This route took him past the farm where the Persson family had lived before moving into town. The place looked pretty much the same as he last remembered; the swing was still in the tree in the front yard. And just as he passed the drive-way, he caught a glimpse of two young boys tossing a stick to a big dog in the farmyard. It was good to know that children lived there, busy making memories as he had done with his family when they lived there.

He soon arrived in St. Peter and turned south towards the grounds of the State Hospital. He wasn't sure where to find his mother so he stopped at the first building inside the gate to inquire about her. He was directed to where she was and once he'd located Building B, he stepped inside to the information desk. A short distance down the hall, he found room 103 and tapped softly on the door. A voice that he didn't recognize called out for him to come in. He opened the door and saw that there were two patients in the room, one sleeping with her face towards the wall. The person who answered identified herself as Mrs. Wagner. Bill told her he was here to see his mother and she suggested that he pull a chair close to Karin's bed so she would see him as soon as she awakened. He did so, sitting there in silence for almost a half hour before Karin turned over, opened her eyes and sat bolt upright in surprise to see Bill by her bedside.

As soon as she recognized him, she began to cry and Bill sat with her on the bed, holding her in his arms, trying to comfort her. But she could not be comforted and the tears went on for a while as he continued to hold her. All of the words he wanted to speak to her went unsaid and all of the difficulties she was experiencing were unspoken also. Finally she was able to stop crying and her first words to him were, "Oh Bill, my dear, dear son. I am so glad to see you." From there on both were able to talk again, Bill sharing news of his life in the Navy, she telling about being in the hospital and how sorry she was to be away from her family.

The time of Bill's visit flew by and soon a nurse came into the room to announce that visiting hours were over for the day. As Bill stood up ready to leave, Karin grabbed his hand, walked with him to the door of the room, gave him one more hug, then asked if he could come back tomorrow. Bill assured her that he would and turned towards the main desk and out the door to the parking lot.

When he got to the car, he sat inside for a few minutes trying to sort out his feelings. It was so good to see his mother again but so worrisome to see her as she now was. He wondered what kind of treatments she was being given and just how long she would remain in the hospital. So many unanswered questions, so little time at home for resolution.

As he drove from the hospital grounds, he glanced back and observed that the whole complex with the high chain link fences that wound around the perimeter, had a forbidding look to it. He rationally understood that some dangerous mental patients had to be confined in this way for their own safety and that of the community. Still he questioned why other patients like his mother were kept in the same prison-like atmosphere. He hurried along the drive back into town, then decided a cold beer might be good after the kind of emotional experience he had while visiting his mother.

The next thing he knew, he was pulling into the parking lot at Hank's, where he and John had stopped last night. He went inside the darkened bar and found a table near the wall. Three or four regular patrons turned to see who came in, then went right back to the beer and conversation at their barstools.

About that time, Annette came from the swinging doors to the kitchen, caught sight of him and walked over to his table. "Well, hello there sailor. We must have impressed you with a good hamburger and beer last night," she said. "Are you back for more of the same?" she questioned. Bill answered, "Just a draft beer for now I guess." She returned with the beer, then noted that he was especially quiet after thanking her for bringing it. Something told her that he needed some quiet understanding so she pulled out another chair from the table and sat down with him. "I'm a good listener if you want to talk," she began. He smiled back at her and soon began sharing the fact that he had just been to see his mother in the State Hospital. Annette listened intently as Bill talked, then told him that she could only imagine how difficult it must have been for him to see his mother where she was.

Her shift was over at 6:00 and a different waitress came on the job. Annette continued to sit with Bill and their conversation went on for a few more minutes. She was so easy to talk to and so understanding of what he had experienced. He was really glad that Annette happened to be at work and they were able to share this emphatic visit.

He mentioned that his brother suggested going to a dance on Saturday night and he asked Annette if she would like to go with them. She said yes and once the plans were made, Bill stood up to leave. She gave him directions to where she lived and he said they would pick her up about 7:30 on Saturday evening.

The drive back to Le Sueur went quickly, and Bill could hardly believe that it was already past seven in the evening. Lars would be home from work and Jana and Lorraine would wonder where he was. On the other hand, the time spent with Annette had been just what he needed and he wasn't going to worry about having missed supper!

The next morning began pretty much the same as the day before. Bill got up and took Lars to work so that he would be able to have the car to get around town. The only difference was that it was Saturday and so, no school for Jana and Lorraine. Jana had a babysitting job with a family in the next block. The Flynn's had three youngsters and their mother was glad when Jana agreed to come to their house and watch her children while she did the weekly housecleaning. She also wanted Jana to stay into the afternoon so that she could go to the grocery store while the children took their naps. Lorraine was going along with Jana to keep her company and to help entertain the Flynn children. Lorraine told Bill that "they had so many toys at that house it was always just like Christmas there." So with his sisters off to baby-sit, Bill decided that before going back to visit his mother, he would stop by the Anderleys to see his baby sister, Katrina.

After driving through downtown Le Sueur, he headed north on Main street and soon spotted the address of 418 Main Street, a short distance past the train depot. He circled around the next block, then parked the car, facing south, directly in front of the Anderley house. He went down several cement steps leading to a sidewalk, and then to a front door entrance.

He knocked at the door and soon Selma Anderley came to the door to see who the visitor was. She opened the door and said, "Hello, there Bill. We heard that you were coming home on leave."

Bill wondered how in the world this information had filtered down to her, but dismissed the question because in small town America all comings and goings were known about. Information about visitors anywhere in town was seldom missed.

"I hope it's all right for me to come to see little Katrina today," Bill began. "I'm only going to be here a short time and I'd really like to see her again."

"Of course it's all right. Come right in and come to the kitchen for some coffee. Katrina and I baked sugar cookies this morning. They're just out of the oven," Selma continued. She led the way through the enclosed front porch, through the living room and dining room back to the kitchen.

"Katrina, look who came to visit us today," Selma said to the little girl who was quietly playing on the kitchen floor with her toy stove and miniature pots and pans. Bill pulled a chair from the kitchen table and leaned over to talk to Katrina who had continued with her play regardless of the visitor in the house.

"Hello there, little sister," Bill said to Katrina. The little girl looked up into her brother's face but didn't recognize or know him. She was now almost two and a half years old and the last time that Bill saw her, Katrina wasn't even a year old and was still living with her family at home.

"I was hoping that you would sit on my lap today and not be frightened of me as you were the last time that I saw you," Bill continued. Selma had poured coffee for she and Bill and brought a cup of milk to the table for Katrina. Sugar cookies were placed on a plate for all to enjoy. Selma picked up Katrina and spoke to her. "Katrina, let's have a cookie and some milk. Your big brother would like a cookie too. Would you give one to him please?" Shyly Katrina took a cookie from the plate and handed it to her brother. "Now would you like to have one too," Selma went on. Katrina took another cookie as Selma sat the child on Bill's lap. "See Katrina, Bill likes the cookies that we made. Aren't you glad we had some to share with him," Selma offered. Bill smiled down on his sister as they all enjoyed their drinks and cookies. Katrina soon decided that Bill was a nice person, and it really was all right to sit on his lap close to him. She leaned her head into his chest, then pulled away again as the wooly feel of his uniform felt scratchy on her cheek.

Selma and Bill continued conversation as they all sat at the table; she sharing how Katrina was doing, he telling where his Navy travels had taken him. A half hour passed by quickly, then Bill said to the little girl on his lap, "It's almost time for me to leave, Katrina, and I'd like to give you a little present to remember me by." He pulled a silver dollar coin from his pocket, then told Katrina that the sailors called these coins "cartwheels" and that she should save it until the next time that she saw him.

As Bill stood up to leave, Katrina reached out towards Selma, a plea to return to someone she called Momma. Selma took Katrina into her arms and walked to the front door with Bill. He leaned forward to give his sister a goodbye kiss, then he went out the door to the car, waving back to Katrina as he left.

Selma found herself with tears in her eyes as Bill drove away from the curb. "What a nice young man your brother is," she spoke to Katrina. "I hope he will be safe from harm and comes back to see us again."

It was just past eleven o'clock by the time Bill turned to cross the bridge leading out of town. He decided against stopping for lunch because he had enjoyed one too many of Selma's cookies and wasn't very hungry just now. The drive to St. Peter took a short time and once he arrived there, it was still much too early for visiting hours at the hospital, so instead, he turned west from town and headed towards the farm where his brother Karl had been employed for several years.

About six miles later, he turned into the lane leading to the Bergerstad place. He pulled to a stop and saw Karl just coming out of the barn. "Hello, brother, Bill," Karl called to him. "I was wondering when I would see you," he continued as he walked to Bill, giving him a brotherly hug and pat on the back. "I was just heading into the house for dinner," Karl continued, "come along with me." "I really don't want to intrude," Bill objected. "Nah, come along with me," Karl countered, "the Bergerstads will feed any stray that shows up at mealtime."

Karl stopped in the back entryway of the house to hang up his work jacket, having already taken off his barn boots on the steps. "Hello, the house," he called into the kitchen. "My brother Bill just stopped by. Is it all right to feed him dinner?" he questioned. Mrs. Bergerstad, a beautiful young blond woman not much older than twenty-five and obviously pregnant, turned towards the door and answered, "Sure Karl. Your brother is welcome. But it means you only get one pork chop instead of two," she teased.

Karl turned towards the sink in the entryway to wash up for dinner and Bill followed his example. After rinsing his hands in the basin of water, Bill pulled the roller towel down to find a dry spot, dried his hands, then followed Karl into the kitchen. Mr. Bergerstad was already seated at the table. He must be at least forty years old Bill decided. A young boy of about three was seated next to Mr. Bergerstad and shyly looked up to see who their visitor was today. He had never before seen someone in uniform and wasn't quite sure if he would like to sit by Bill or not.

As soon as introductions were made, Karl, Bill and Frances Bergerstad seated themselves at the table. It was not routine for this family to offer a prayer at mealtime. Instead, as soon as Henry Bergerstad had helped himself to the first pork chop off the platter, the rest of the food was passed around and eating began. The little boy, Ronnie, could not keep his eyes off of Bill.

Bill sensed the child's curiosity and broke the silence in the room by saying to him, "I see that you are interested in my uniform. I am a sailor and I work and live on a ship. I like to wear my blue uniform when I am visiting friends. Do you think you could be my friend?" After a quick nod indicating yes, the child turned back to his meal.

As soon as Henry had finished eating, he noisily shoved his chair away from the table and left the room. All the others at the table continued their meal, and then as Bill rose, he picked up his plate, cup and silverware and carried them to the kitchen sink. "Thank you very much for allowing me to enjoy this delicious meal with your family," he said to Frances. She smiled at him and said, "You are most welcome. I hope you will come again."

Karl stood up with Bill and said, "I'm going outside with my brother for a while before he leaves."

The two brothers sat in the car talking for a while, then Karl said, "Well, I guess I really should get back to work. They're not paying me for conversation around here." Bill's final words to Karl that day were, "That little Ronnie reminds me so much of the picture that the folks have of you at that age, Karl." Karl gave a little smile but did not offer an answer.

The drive back to St. Peter, then to the State Hospital faded into a blur as Bill drove to his destination, scarcely even seeing the passing scenery along the way. He parked the car and went directly into the building where Karin was. He walked towards her room, pausing a moment for a quick hello to the nurse at the desk as he went by. He found Karin, sitting in a chair, reading a book as he entered her room.

"Hi, Mom. How's it going today," he asked as he planted a kiss on her cheek. Karin quickly set the book down and rose to collect a hug from her son. "I'm doing just fine today. How could it be any other way with my dear son here to see me," she went on.

Bill was amazed at the change in his mother from the previous day's visit. Today she was the mother he remembered; smiling at him, teasing him about his dimples, asking about how his life was now. Bill contemplated how difficult it was to traverse the ups and downs of depression, not only for the person involved, but also for those who stood by with love, struggling to understand. Together Bill and Karin laughed and talked their way through their visit until, much too soon, the nurse came back to Karin's room saying that visiting hours were now over.

As Bill embraced his mother one last time for the day, he said to her, "Dad and I and the girls will come back to see you tomorrow."

"Oh, good," Karin answered, "it's been a while since Jana and Lorraine were here. I'm anxious to see them again."

Later that afternoon when Bill arrived home again, he found that Jana and Lorraine were back from the day's babysitting job. They were glad to see him there and enjoyed some sibling time together that included a rousing game of Rook.

When Jana looked at the kitchen clock and saw that it was almost five thirty, she said, "It's time to get supper ready. Dad will be home soon. How about some fried eggs and pancakes?" Bill and Lorraine agreed that would make a good supper and they helped Jana by getting the table set. Everything was ready for their meal when Lars arrived home at six from work.

They had just begun the meal when John walked in the door. "Is there enough for me?" he questioned. "I can put some more eggs on," Jana offered and rose to prepare them.

"Let me take over, Sis," Bill said. "I've prepared eggs for over one hundred sailors. Taking care of just one hungry brother will be easy!"

They continued the meal with happy banter back and forth, sharing what each had done that day. "John and I will do the dishes tonight," Bill spoke up to say when the meal was over. The girls and Lars went into the living room, turned on the radio and began enjoying some music before it was time for the Lux Radio Theater. When John and Bill had finished cleaning up the kitchen, Bill went upstairs to change from his uniform to civilian clothes. He spoke to John as he came back into the living room saying, "I've been in my blues all day and it's time to go "off duty."

The brothers said good-bye to everyone, then left the house to drive to Annette's home to pick her up as planned. She answered Bill's knock on the door, called a quick goodbye to her parents, then the three young people proceeded on their way to the Mankato Ballroom for an evening of dancing.

"Looks like a good crowd tonight," John said as he maneuvered into a parking spot. "I know that some of our old gang will be here.

Fred Schmidt and Evelyn for sure." He went on to name several others that enjoyed going to dances. Bill was anxious to get into the ballroom to see them for himself.

Once inside, John spotted several tables pushed together where Fred and Evelyn were sitting with Katie, Don Mueller and several others. He led the way to the group, ahead of Bill and Annette. Fred jumped up as soon as he saw Bill and quickly found three more chairs to seat the newcomers. All the people were excited to see Bill again. The conversation was lively and animated as everyone wanted to hear from him about his Navy experiences.

The band returned from their break and again the music started up. Bill got to his feet and led Annette to the dance floor. "I don't even know if I remember how to dance," he apologized to her as they took their first few steps to the music. "We'll figure it out together," she answered. Soon they were waltzing around the floor, not really caring if the dance they were doing was right or not! It was fun and they just laughed when one or the other stepped on a misplaced toe. Several polka sets followed, then Bill and Annette returned to the table to sit for a while to catch their breath and cool off with a bottle of beer.

The evening went on happily; Bill enjoyed dancing with his friends Evelyn and Katie. John and Fred whirled Annette around the floor also. John was a very good dancer and never was at a loss for a partner. Women that he didn't even know would ask him to dance and he did enjoy that kind of attention! Several times a young man came to the table to ask Annette to dance. She got up once to do a set with him, but when he came back the next time, she declined. Bill noticed her sitting alone at the table and guided his partner Evelyn back to the table so that Annette would not be alone. Evelyn excused herself go to the restroom and Bill and Annette sat together at the table talking. "Are you having a good time," Bill asked her. "Well, yes, I was until Harry came by. We have dated a time or two but when I found out that he drank so much, I broke it off. Now he wants to see me again," Annette explained. "Well, you'll just have to tell him that you found a new boyfriend," Bill said. "Oh, my goodness," Annette stammered. "I've seen you twice at Hanks, here we are at a dance and now you are my boyfriend?" she questioned. "That comment just kind of flew out of my mouth," Bill answered. "I hope I haven't offended you," he added. Annette rose from her chair, took Bill by the hand and changed the subject by leading him to the dance floor.

Much too soon the last dance was called, and after finishing one final turn around the floor, everyone returned to their tables. John announced that he, Don, Katie and a girl from Cleveland would ride home together and that Bill could take his car and see Annette home. That settled, everyone left the ballroom and headed their respective ways.

Bill and Annette continued chatting along the way home. They both found it so easy to communicate with the other one and were disappointed when the ride ended so quickly.

"Would you like to come in for a sandwich or something," Annette asked Bill. "That sounds great. Are you sure your folks won't mind a strange guy in their kitchen at this time of the night?

Bill questioned. He went on to add, "I'd hate to get off on the wrong foot with your Dad."

Once inside the kitchen, Annette set out left over roast beef and a loaf of homemade bread. She prepared the sandwiches and they sat at down the kitchen table to enjoy their snack. Once again they got all caught up in conversation as they grew better acquainted with each other. Then, oblivious of the passing time, they heard the clock in the living room struck three.

"I had no idea it was this late, Annette," Bill began. "I should be getting home before John rolls in," he added.

Annette walked out on the back porch to say good night to Bill, and before either of them knew what happened, they found themselves in each other's arms. It followed naturally that several kisses followed. Stepping back for a breath, Bill could only say, "I really didn't intend for that to happen so quickly." Annette quickly assured him that she didn't either but that it just felt like the thing to do. She went on to say that she hoped she could see him again while he was still at home on leave. He assured her that she was going to be a big part of the rest of his time in Le Sueur!

On the drive home, Bill tried to sort out what was happening with he and Annette. He really had no intention of getting close to another girl so soon after his bad experience with Paula. He thought he had steeled himself against another relationship, but along came Annette and all his resolve disappeared. He made his way into the house and upstairs to the bedroom to find John sprawled in the bed. "Hey, little brother. Give me my half of the bed," he whispered to John. John turned over on his side and Bill eased into bed, certain that he was not going to be able to sleep anyway.

The next thing that Bill was aware of was sounds coming from downstairs. It was morning much too soon and John was up fixing coffee. Bill heard Jana and Lorraine in the kitchen too. Soon he heard his Dad's voice there also and he grudgingly got up himself. By the time he had put on his shirt and trousers and came downstairs, Lars and John had toast and oatmeal ready to put on the table.

"Well, good morning, sunshine," John greeted his brother. "Are you up for all day?" he teased. After a quick nod, Bill found a place at the table and soon everyone was enjoying their breakfast.

When all had finished, Lars proposed that they all ride together to the hospital to see Karin that afternoon. Sunday visiting hours were extended and began at 1:00 instead of 2:00 and he wanted to spend as much time with her as they could on that day.

Just before one o'clock, the whole family was walking into Building B at the State Hospital, making their way down the hall to room 103. As they neared the door, they could hear voices coming from the room. Bill recognized Mrs. Wagner's voice from his previous visit and he surmised the other voice was from a nurse who was in the room to assess the situation. Both women seemed to be trying their best to calm Karin who was crying loudly and uncontrollably. Lars turned to his family and suggested they wait outside the door for just a minute as he went in first to see Karin. The sobbing noise continued as he came out to rejoin his children.

"Dad, how about if I try calm Mom down," Bill asked. Lars said that he should try and Bill went into the room. When Karin saw him, she seemed like she wanted to settle down but just could not right away. Bill sat holding her in his arms as he had done on his first visit, and a few minutes later, the crying stopped.

"The girls came to see you today, Mom," Bill said. "Would you like to have them come in now?" he questioned. Karin said that she was so lonesome for her little girls and yes, they could come right in. Bill waved through the doorway to Lars who came into the room with Jana and Lorraine. John followed them dispiritedly. The nurse led Mrs. Wagner from the room to give the family privacy, and once they were gone, it was easier for everyone to join in conversation.

Karin seemed anxious to have Lorraine sit on her lap, but Lorraine held back from her mother and did not want to be that close. Jana sat down next to her mother and held her hand. The conversation went reasonably well for a few minutes, then without warning, Karin began to sob again. No matter how her family tried to comfort her, she could not stop crying.

At that, Lorraine joined in with tears of her own. "I want to go home now," she wailed. Lars announced that all would be leaving and that they would try to visit on another day. Bill felt so bad about leaving Karin in this situation, but it did appear hopeless for today as Lars had said. As he went out the door, he called back to his mother that he would come to visit again on Tuesday. The sadly dejected family made their way out of the building to the car.

Jana and Lorraine were especially quiet on the way home again until Bill suggested that they stop for an ice cream cone in Le Sueur. Even Lars perked up at that suggestion. John turned into a parking space in front of Braun's café and the whole family went inside. Bill, Lars and John decided to have pie and coffee but the girls held fast to the suggestion of ice cream cones. Soon everyone was enjoying their treat, smiling and enjoying a good time once again. Everyone agreed that Bill's idea to stop was sure a good one!

Bill returned to see his mother again on Tuesday as he had promised to do and went back again for a short visit on Wednesday also. Both visits were a repeat of what he had experienced previously; one time Karin was her old self, smiling and joking with him, the next, she was crying uncontrollably. It was an emotional roller-coaster for sure. If it had not been for the several more times he was able to be with Annette, Bill would have wanted to leave sooner. But as it was, he really didn't want to leave at all.

Thursday was the last night of his leave at home. John, Karl and Anna, along with her family, came to the Persson home that evening to share a dessert that Anna had made. Bill invited Annette to come also. He wanted his new friend to meet his dad and his other siblings. John volunteered to pick Annette up on his way from Cleveland and also assured Bill that he could use the car to take her home again.

There were smiling faces all around; from Anna's young children to Lars, who was enjoying his children and grandchildren in a happy setting. If only Karin could have been there with them.

As planned, John came back early Friday morning to take Bill to meet his train in Mankato. The girls were already off to school and Lars for work, when John came into the house. Bill was sitting at the kitchen table enjoying a final cup of coffee at home before it was time to leave.

"Well, big brother, are you ready to travel again?" questioned John. "Yes, I'm ready to get back and see where I'll be going next. Probably back to Hawaii again I think," Bill answered.

Bill got up from his chair, put his cup in the sink and slung his sea bag over his shoulder. "Let's weigh anchor, matey," he teased John. John gave him a salute and answered, "Aye, aye, sir." Their banter continued back and forth until they arrived at the Mankato train station. "Just drop me off here," Bill said. "You don't need to come into the station with me. I know that Mr. Wolf wants you back on the job this afternoon." "No rest for the wicked, dear brother," John answered.

Once inside the station, Bill found the right gate for the train that would take him to Omaha, Denver, Los Angeles and his final destination, San Diego. He found an empty seat, stowed his bag, sat down and in a very short time, was fast asleep.

***

U.S.S. Preston #379
Pear Harbor, Hawaii
Oct. 23, 1940
Dear Mother,
I'm back in Hawaii again now. 5,000 miles from Le Sueur, which isn't so far away at that when you think of it. Only took 11 days from the time I left Le Sueur until I got here.

I met another sailor on the train, going through Nebraska, who I know. So when we got to Los Angeles, Calif Sunday morning, we went up to his brother's home and had breakfast. Then took a bath and stayed there the rest of the day just resting up after that long train ride. Had a nice trip all the way.

Took the eight o'clock train from L.A. to San Diego that evening and got there at 11:00 P.M. I returned to the ship and checked in, as I had to be back at mid-night.

We left San Diego in the afternoon of Mon. the 14th. Were en-route a week, arrived at Pearl Harbor the day before yesterday, Mon. the 21st. The ocean was pretty rough all the way back, but then that's to be expected this time of the year.

We went into port upon arrival. Fueled ship and then put out to sea again. Expect we will be at sea until about November 1ˢᵗ. Then we are supposed to go alongside the dock for 3 weeks. Which will be pretty nice. From what I hear we are supposed to have magnetic mine cables put on our ship at that time. It certainly is hot down here after being up in Minnesota and seeing white frost a couple mornings. I haven't been ashore yet since we came back but I expect old Honolulu is just the same as it ever was.

There are several thousand new men in the navy now. And the ships are getting pretty well filled up. We have about 30 more on now than we had before. That makes it better because there are that many more to help with the work.

We fire 10 practice rounds of anti-aircraft tomorrow. On Friday we fire 60 shells anti-aircraft. Getting a lot of gun practice lately. From what it looks like I think we well be in Hawaiian waters for quite some time yet.

I wish I could have stayed home longer this time, but I was glad I had the chance to get back for even a week. I'll try to get leave again to come home the next time we go back to Calif. Maybe then I can get a longer leave.

Hope you are feeling better Mother dear. I had a cold when I left but got over it right away.

Must stop now, will write again soon. All my love.   Your son, Bill

***

Bill sent several more letters to his mother and sister in November of 1940, sharing with them what had transpired since his return to the Preston after his leave. Most all of his time was now spent on duty in the fire room. When he stood watch late evening to early morning, he brought along his writing tablet and pen. Since this particular duty was pretty routine, he was able to compose letters written from below deck in the power section of the Preston. His on duty hours varied from standing watch to having hands on experience in learning how to power up the engines and maintain them to rigid Navy standards. He did enjoy being a part of the "black gang" and being in the fire-room of the ship. It appeared to Bill that the chances for advancement and pay raises were more available in the "black gang" and these incentives added to his dream of being a success in what he was doing.

***

...............Should have written long before but somehow the days slip into weeks and I just didn't get down to it. I wrote to Anna some time ago so she should have gotten my letter by now........

..............I wish I could have stayed at home longer than I did. Probably next year I'll be able to get 30 days leave. If I do, I'll come home for awhile again......................

.............We've had patrol for the past week at the island of Maui. We're anchored over the weekend about a mile offshore. I went ashore with a bunch of the boys yesterday and played softball almost all afternoon. Sure was fun to get off the ship and get some exercise. Then in the evening a friend and I went swimming off the dock for a couple of hours. More fun than a barrel of monkeys. Have to be back to the ship at 7:00 PM at this island. On weekends liberty starts at 1 PM if we're at anchor......

.........guess I'll go ashore again this afternoon and go for a hike. It's pretty nice over here as far as Hawaii goes. Cane fields, hibiscus flowers and of course the inevitable palm trees. We aren't allowed to carry cameras around the islands anymore since the war is going on, so can't take any snapshots......................

............Ever see Annette around? I wrote to her a while back so expect to get a letter from her soon...................

…………Suppose John and Karl are still picking corn. Say hello to them and Dad from me………….

………Sincerely hope you are improving, Mother. Wish I could be able to see you once in a while. But since that is impossible, I'll have to send you my love by mail………..

***

U.S. S. Preston
Pearl Harbor, Hawaii
Nov. 24, 1940
Dear Karl,
Your letter arrived a few days ago so I guess it's time I scribbled a few lines in return.

The good ship Preston is now alongside the destroyer tender U.S. S. Dixie in Pearl Harbor. We've been here now for a couple weeks for over-haul period. It's pretty nice not to have to be at sea for a while. Although there is a lot of work to do while in port.

Last weekend I went out to the navy recreation camp over Sat & Sun. It's near Manakuli beach. Nice place out there. Just loafed, swam and sun bathed. Had a good beer party in the evening. Came back to the ship, Monday, with sand in my hair and a beautiful case of sunburn. My first job when I got back was to scrape and paint bilges in the fire-room. There's just barely enough room enough to squirm around there under the boilers and floor plates. Which considering my sunburn was very refined torture.

Went ashore over to Honolulu last Mon evening. Bought a few things including a birthday present for Mother. Also made out a money order to Jana and Lorraine…

I brought my civilian clothes back with me from San Diego this time. Went ashore last night and rented a locker on the beach to keep them. We aren't allowed to have civilian clothes aboard ship. It costs me $3.00 a *month for a locker. They sure know how to charge for everything out here. Back in the States I had a good locker for $1.00 a month.*

A couple other fellows and I went on a "blitzkreig" last night in Honolulu. But we had to be back at the ship 1:00 o'clock in the morning. So a guy doesn't hardly get a chance to get started before you have to go back again.

Our ship goes into dry dock this coming Wednesday. We'll be there a day or two. Scrape and paint the entire bottom of this pig-iron bean-barge.

We have a new uniform now to wear aboard ship after working hours in the tropics. Instead of wearing long white trousers we have white shorts. They are a lot cooler and easier to keep clean as well.........

Even got a letter from Annette not so long ago. Hope to hear from her again...............

Glad to hear that you missed the draft but suppose you'll be drafted sooner or later anyhow. Well after all a year isn't so long. I've been in the navy two years now by next month.

Greetings to all the family from me and don't forget to write once in a while. After all it doesn't take long to write a letter.

Your Brother Bill

***

U.S.S. Preston
Pearl Harbor, Hawaii
Dec. 22, 1940
Dear Mother,

It's been nearly three weeks ago since I wrote to you last so will attempt to compose a letter now. Don't know if you received my other letters or not. The only mail I've had from home in the last two months in a letter from Anna and a card and letter from Karl. I wish Jana would write.

Well it's soon Christmas again, next Wednesday. This will be the second Christmas I'm spending in Hawaii. Don't suppose it will be much different from last year. I have the duty Christmas Eve until noon Christ-

mas day. Probably will go ashore to Honolulu and go to church in the evening.

Things go on the same as ever in the navy. In port a few days, then out to sea again for a while. Battle practice and dry dock. I'm in good health and hope this finds you improved.

Must be very cold back in Minn. from what I hear over the radio. I got a letter from Ed Swansons in Nov. and Helen sent some clippings from the St. Peter Herald about the early blizzard they had. One thing we don't have to worry about in Hawaii. The weather is just like summer here.

Had a letter from Vivian a while back. She's working in Chicago again now. Also had a couple letters from Annette.

We stripped ship last week. That is they took off all unnecessary equipment to make the ship lighter. Also combustibles such as wood. And glass articles that weren't needed. I guess it's just another drill.

I'm writing this after the movie this evening. It's about 9:15 P.M. Sunday night. The name of the show was "Three Cheers for the Irish." I thought it was pretty good.

I have the watch in the boiler room from midnight until 4:00 o'clock tomorrow morning so I guess I should get to bed and get some sleep.

Hope you have a nice Christmas. Any may 1941 bring you much happiness, Mother dear.

Give my best regard to all the family.

Your loving son, Bill

***

USS Preston
Jan. 9, 1941
Dear Jana,

How's the world treating you? Was glad to hear from you again. Almost thought you had forgotten me.

Well, things go on the same as usual down here on "the Rock." Work five days a week and go ashore occasionally. Our ship has been in port quite a bit lately. It's a nice rest after being at sea a lot.

Went to church last Sunday at the Lutheran Church in Honolulu. Went to the band concert at Kapiolani Park the Sunday before. They have a band they call the Royal Hawaiians. They played a lot of old favorites like the Blue Danube Waltz. Remember you used to play that on the phonograph all the time?

Went to the aquarium(don't know if that's spelled right) some time ago. Saw several hundred different kinds of fish, eels, and turtles. Some of these tropical fish are very beautiful. All colors of the rainbow.

Things are pretty dull around Honolulu as far as recreation is concerned. Going to movies is about all there usually is to do over there. Our ship threw a beer party the 30th of December but it turned out to be a fizzle.

Received a letter from Annette yesterday. She keeps me posted on all the latest scandal in Le Sueur. Am writing to her tonight too.

Where's Dad working now days? Give him my regards. Got a letter from Otto a few days ago.......

I guess I'll write to Mother soon again too. The last time I wrote was about 2 weeks ago. Does she come home very often?

Time to go to bed now, so as the Hawaiians say, "Aloha!" Don't wait as long as you did last time before answering.

Your loving brother, Bill

***

U. S. S. Preston #379
Pearl Harbor, Hawaii
Feb. 5 1941
Dear Mother,

I have been going to write for such a long time but it seems I just keep putting it off....... Seems there's never anything to write about.

My ship was alongside the dock for a few weeks during Dec. & Jan. We had degaussing cables put on. They are used to repel magnetic mines.

During the time we were in port I went over to visit Bill Strand on the U. S. S. Warrington on Sunday. Had a nice long talk with him. He's Sea. 1/c striking for torpedo man 3/c. While I was over there I also met a fellow from Winnebago, Minn. I was in the same C.C.C. camp with him out in Washington in 1936. Quite a surprise to see him again. The last time I saw him was in '37 nearly 2,000 miles from Minn. And now I meet him again down here in Honolulu 3,000 miles from Wash. It's a small world.

Went to sea two weeks ago and have been in port only a couple days since then. Every night at sunset all the lights on the whole ship are turned off for "darken ship" while at sea, so it gets pretty tiresome with nothing to do in the evening.

We had plane guard for the U. S. S. Yorktown for a week. Quite interesting to watch the planes take off and land on her deck. Also watched the dive bombers bomb & target and torpedoes fired from torpedo planes.

Our ship fired two depth charges last week. That's the first time we've fired any since I came aboard. They're used as a weapon against submarines. We drop them into the water to a depth of about 150 ft. before they explode. They have each 600 lbs. Of TNT in them so you can imagine what an explosion it makes.

At sea we stand watches in the fire-room 4 hours on and 8 hrs. off so we have quite a bit of time off. But there's nothing to do when we're off duty. The rocking, rolling motion of the ship gets tiring. Most of the time I have off at sea I sleep.

We came into port today again. We'll be in now for about 3 wks. Alongside the destroyer U.S.S. Whitney for overhaul.

We're going to tear down two boilers and overhaul them during that time. At least I'll have plenty work to do and the time will pass a little faster.

I wish I could go back to California but it doesn't look very promising.

I got a card from Mrs. Ed Swanson today, also a letter from Annette a couple days ago...............

Your loving son, Bill

***

The Preston continued maneuvers in and out of Hawaii during the first months of 1941. The United States stayed hopeful that the war situation going on in the world would not involve them, but at the same time they remained watchful of the Japanese advancements in the Pacific, and simultaneously kept an eye on the European situation with the advancement of the Nazi takeover going on there. As the United States watched, they prepared. All the maneuvers and training going on within the Navy, added to their expertise and strength on the seas.

Bill's comments about having the ship darkened in the evening, a boring, bothersome experience for him, was in actuality a necessary training experience to learn how to move about the waters under cover of night. Unfortunately these maneuvers were not without expense. In March of 1941, four destroyers that were involved in nighttime movements collided. Most damages were repairable, but there was also loss of life.

***

U. S. S. Preston –379-
Pearl Harbor, Hawaii
April 14, 1941
My dear Mother,
I have been intending to write for such a long time but it seems something always comes up to keep me from it. We have been at sea nearly all the time for over a month and it's next to impossible to write then because

*it's so rough. Almost like trying to write when you're riding in a car. We came into port last Wed the 9*th *however so I will have to catch up on all the letters I owe. We went alongside the repair ship this morning for a ten day emergency overhaul. It's a relief to be able to go ashore again for a change. Also to have movies in the evening and lights on the ship. We don't have either of the two when at sea during night.*

Hope you received the Easter card I sent, also the Mother's Day card and the $5.00. I sent the last to your Le Sueur address so you would be sure to get it. You'll probably get it a couple days after you receive this.

Yesterday was Easter Sunday. I wanted to go to church in the morning at Honolulu, but there was some urgent work that had to be done, so had to stay aboard and work all day. I did go over last night though after we finished with the job and had a very nice evening.

Everything goes on the same as ever out here. Only we are preparing for war more than at any time before. Looks like we might get a sample of it yet before it's over. I'd just as soon get in it and have it out then to have to keep on waiting the way we have been doing since it started in 1939.

Got a letter from Anna a few days ago...............

*It's Lorraine's birthday the 6*th *of next month so I sent her a birthday card and $5.00 so she can buy anything she needs as a birthday present. Also sent Jana $5.00 and Dad $10.00. Hope they get it O.K.*

Tomorrow is my payday again so I guess I'll send some money for my church dues at St. Peter. I owe $15.00. I want to keep up my church membership because I may go back there to live someday. Things are so unsettled now that I don't have any definite plans for the future. I may have to stay in the navy for a while after my enlistment is up. But that is still a year and a half from now so there's no use in crossing bridges before you get there.

I have an allotment made out to the Bank of America at San Diego for $20.00 a month. It's only been in effect for 2 ½ months so I haven't but $50.00 saved up as yet. Still it counts up some, and I'll always have it in case of emergency or a little nest egg saved up by the time my cruise is over.

I'm getting along fine in the boiler room. Haven't been sick a day since I was home last fall.

We worked all day today repairing the boilers. Have about another week yet to overhaul them. Had the duty tonight so stayed aboard. I rate liberty at 3:00 o'clock tomorrow afternoon so guess I'll browse over to town have a couple beers and see a movie. Have to get a haircut too before my hair gets so long it curls up in back like a duck's tail.

I bought a pair of gray shoes the other day for $4.85 to wear with my civilian clothes. I have gray slacks and sport coat. The shoes are two-tone. Look almost like that pair I bought when I was working at Wettergren's in 1938.

I'm sending a picture of myself and a shipmate taken with a "Hawaiian girl!" Thought you'd like it.

Must say good-bye for this time.

Your loving son, Bill

***

U.S.S. Preston –379-
Pearl Harbor, Hawaii
April 21, 1941
Dear Karl,

I've owed you a letter now for the last two months so I'd better get down to writing it or I never will get it answered. But then it usually takes you that long to answer as well so that makes it mutual.

This letter will hardly reach you in time for your birthday but nevertheless my sincere wishes for many happy returns of the day.

There isn't much to write about as we aren't supposed to mention anything about movements of naval vessels or anything that pertains to armament of ships. So that doesn't leave me much to write about. However I can say that we have spent more time at sea continuously in the past two months than for anytime before the same length of time.

Our ship came into port the 9th of Apr. for general overhaul and we have been in since then. Are supposed to go out again the 23rd and I don't know where we go from here. There have been a lot of rumors around but nothing definite. If we go to some foreign port I'll let you know about it.

There were about a dozen destroyers and cruisers that were down in Australia and New Zealand for a while but they came back the other day. Wish this bean barge would make a trip down there. She hasn't been there since 1936.

I've sure been catching up on my liberties in Honolulu the past two weeks. I go over every time I get a chance. Had a Hawaiian waitress out last night. She was homely as a mud wall ……

Didn't get to go ashore Easter Sunday. Had to work all day loading ammunition.

The U.S.S. Warrington was in a collision here some time ago with another destroyer, but I see they have her back in commission again now. Nobody hurt. Two other destroyers collided the same night during black-out maneuvers. One guy burned to death on one of them. We could see the fire a long way off. Saw them in dry- dock afterwards. Reminds you of a 1941 Model car that got wrapped around a tree.

A sailor and a soldier got in a fight last Wednesday night in a joint uptown. The "dog-face" had a knife and the "gob" didn't. They carried the sailor out feet first, dead as a dodo bird. Seems like the Army and Navy boys get into it every once in a while.

The night before last I was coming back to the yard in a taxi. I saw two sailors who were riding a motorcycle that hit a bus head on. They were covered with sheets when I got there. They're being sent back to the U.S. in wooden overcoats!!

We are over at the Naval Ammunition depot again today and have some sort of electrical gadget hooked up to the ship to magnetize her. I don't savy it but it has something to do with these new magnetic mines.

A bunch of us went over to the yard canteen tonight and took on a few cool Budweisers. Tasted pretty good after standing a watch in the fireroom at 117°.

I'm in the best of health and hope this finds you the same. Give my regards to John. And say hello to Annette if you see her.

Sincerely, Bill

***

The April 1941 letters to Karin and Karl were followed with a letter to Jana on May 25,1941.

***

U. S. S. Preston –379-
Pearl Harbor, Hawaii
Dear Sis,

I'm ashamed of my laziness. I should have written a long time ago…. Was glad to hear from you. You're the only one from back home that ever writes anymore. You and Annette……

As ever there's hardly anything to write about. Besides the usual stuff. War games and war news. That's all you ever hear or read about anymore is war. I wish we would get in it and get it over with. Staying out here and waiting for something to happen in like waiting for a century plant to bloom……

The funny part of it is I'll probably wind up by doing twenty years in the navy for a pension just like thousands of other sailors who swore they wouldn't stay in the navy over four years. And then were afraid to leave the outfit and make a fresh start in civilian life.

I finally made fireman 1ˢᵗ class so I draw $60.00 a month now. In another year I should be getting $72 a month if I pass the exams for water tender. That's the way it goes. A fellow doesn't want to leave a steady income and gamble on a chance of getting steady work on the outside. I've *just got 18 more months to do till I get paid off. Then if I'm water tender 2/c and agree to extend my cruise for two more years I'll get $200 shipping over money and another $100 transportation money. Also an $8.00 a month increase in pay. Well, $300 isn't exactly "hay."*

Spend most of the time at sea now. Darken ship every night. Manuevers and more maneuvers. Gets pretty tiresome after a while. I went ashore last Sat. night as we came into Pearl Harbor again last Fri. First time I have left the ship for over a month. And sweetheart, good old mother earth feels pretty nice under a man's feet after walking a destroyer deck at sea for a long time.

Will be in port for some time now, a couple weeks for overhaul, then out to sea again for another stretch. I worked all day tearing down boilers in the fire room. Not so bad though. I like to work with machinery. Take it apart and put it back together again.

.... Now that mother is home again I pray that she will be able to stay home and things will work out for the better....give her my love.

.............Give my best regards to all the folks. I'm in the best of health and hope this finds you the same. Cheerio. I'll be seein' you all in a year or two...........

Your loving brother, Bill

***

When Karin was released from the hospital to come home in May of 1941, Lars was hopeful that he, the girls and Karin could settle down into being a regular family again. Jana and Lorraine were overjoyed to have their mother back with them. Jana had become the mother figure in the household during the time that Karin was hospitalized; now she could look forward to being a carefree young girl again, not the one in charge of her sister, and so much of the daily demands of running a house. The possibility of bringing Katrina back home was talked about, but Lars felt that Karin should have some additional time with just he and the older girls before bringing a busy little three year old back into the picture. He saw Katrina occasionally and observed how happy she seemed to be living with the Anderleys. They had agreed that she could continue to stay there at least for a while longer as Karin continued her recovery during the transition period between hospital and home.

So just the four of them became a family again, with regular visits from John and sporadic visits from Karl. Anna and her family stopped by often. Karin was delighted to have her grandchildren come and looked forward to all of their visits.

In early June after school was out for the year, a family who had been country neighbors of the Perssons asked if Jana could stay with them for the summer to care for their children and help out around the house as needed. Of course Jana jumped at the chance to earn some money and experience what it was like living someplace other than at home. She would be able to come back home every Sunday so she would still see the family often. Lorraine was not sure that she could handle being without her sister but on the other hand, the prospect of having Karin all to herself was appealing. It had been really difficult for this eleven year old to be without her mother all those weeks that Karin was gone.

Once again a valise was packed; this time a Persson daughter left to be away from home for a while to find out what it would be like to be someone's "hired girl." A short time later, Jana wrote to Bill telling him about her job and how much she was enjoying her adventure.

***

U.S.S. Preston
July 24, 1941
Dear Jana, (c/o Clarence Rethwill)
Thanks for the interesting letter I received a couple days ago. I was beginning to wonder how everything was back there.

It's been quite a while since I last wrote but since the Navy censorship went into effect a couple of months ago, we aren't allowed to write about much that goes on down here on "the rock."

Having warm weather down here too. Almost like the summers in Minn. It's fairly cool when we are at sea, that is on the topside. It's never cool in the fire room. Usually way over 110' or more.

A fellow on our ship was home on leave for 45 days at Austin, Minn. Just got back yesterday. He said the boys that got drafted are "singing the blues." Wonder what their tune would be if they had a 4 yr. stretch to do, instead of 12 months.

I'm in a kind of cramped position to be writing. I'm sitting on a gun platform on the fantail. We're allowed to use the mess tables when writing but the mess compartments are too hot for comfort. I stay above deck as much as possible.

I haven't written to Anna for ages. I really must write to her soon. Sorry to hear that little Anna and Eddie had whooping cough. But then of course that's to be expected sooner or later nearly everyone has it. I remember how sick Lorraine was that Xmas I came home when I was working for Ed Swanson……

I'm not allowed to write about how much time we are at sea or in port. These are times of war, and of course we have to take pre-cautions. However I'm getting along about the same as ever. And the Islands haven't changed much except that there are more people coming down here every day. Suppose I might enjoy it under different circumstances. The tourists at least claim that the Islands are the most beautiful place they've ever seen. I've yet to meet a service man who would say that.

I was delighted with the snapshots you sent. Thanks a lot.

It's nice to know that you're getting along O.K. at the place you're working. Hope you'll be able to go to high school and finish.

Had a letter from Annette yesterday. She sent me a graduation photo of herself. Told me she intended to go to school another year and then teach school.

Suppose nearly all the farmers are done threshing by now. I would have liked to have come home on leave this summer. But that's out of the question. Perhaps I may be able to wrangle a leave before my cruise is up in another year and 5 months.

It's about 6:00 PM now. The evening newspapers should be aboard by now. Guess I'll buy one and see how the Russians and "Krauts" are making out. Mostly though I'll buy it to work the crossword puzzle. I had to get up at 4:00 this morning so it's been a long day.

Well guess I'll drop down to the fire-room and have a cup of "Janoke"(coffee to you) before the movies. We have free movies nearly every night so that helps pass the time away.

When you see the family, give them all my best regards. I'm feeling as fit as ever.

Your loving brother, Bill

***

In early August, Bill sent $10 to Jana for her birthday. It was hard for him to believe that Jana was now fourteen years old. Those years between the day this newborn sister was brought home from the hospital, to 1941, went past so quickly.

Annette also had an August birthday and Bill sent her a small wooden chest in which to keep miscellaneous "treasures". He wondered if she cared to keep his letters to her. The ones sent to him did so much to boost his morale while he was thousands of miles from home. They had become regular correspondents and grew better acquainted through their writings. If only they were nearer, this friendship could develop further. But for now, there were no commitments binding them. Bill still enjoyed taking a girl out when he was in port and he felt sure that Annette was still a regular with the crowd back home.. He hated the idea of some other guy dating her, but was certain that someone as lovely as she, was never hard up for a dancing or skating partner! She would be going to school in fall for her teacher's degree and that would fill a great deal of her time too. They would just have to continue being friends by mail.

***

U.S. S. Preston #379

September 8, 1941

Dear Sis Jana,

A mail ship leaves for the states today. This letter may or may not get on it. I'm writing this on watch in the fire room during the few minutes I have off from firing the boiler and watching a dozen gages.

Received your letter. Also the first copy of the Le Sueur Herald. Thanks a lot for having it sent to me. I subscribed to it the first year I was in the navy but when it ran out, I never renewed it. Made me just a little home-sick to read the familiar names of the people and places back there.

I expect to get a couple weeks leave and come home again for a visit either next month or in November. I'm not sure yet but if things work out the way I think they will, I'm pretty sure I'll be able to. That's about all I can tell you because they are so strict about what we write since the war started. Not allowed to tell you what we've been doing lately, but it's about the same old routine as ever.

By now you will be attending high school. I'm sure glad that you have this privilege. I wish I would have been able to go. Never realized how much I missed until the last couple years. It's a largely competitive world and the fellow with an education is the guy who is on top regardless of where he is or what duty he has.

I get regular letters from Annette as you know. She is studying to become a school teacher and by now she should be attending "normal" at Le Center. It was her birthday the 28th of August. She's just 4 years older than you and 4 years younger than I.

The weather has been disagreeably warm this summer down here, but of course it doesn't go to extremes like back in Minnesota. Usually it's around 80' in summer and 70' in winter. You don't hardly know when the seasons change down here. But the schools in Honolulu change their sports with the seasons just like they do back in the states. Saw some boys starting football practice the other day so I guess fall is here. I guess the reason they follow the same routine as the States is because some schools back there come out to play against them. High schools and colleges from Calif. and other states come out here to compete in baseball, basketball and football. Suppose you'll become quite a basketball fan like most high school girls are. Le Sueur usually has a quite a good team too.

Had another letter from Lorraine and one from Mother the other day. Was so glad to hear from her. It's the first I've gotten since I was home on leave last year.

Hope John is still around by the time I get home so I can see him again before he joins the Army. I wish he would have joined the navy instead at the same time I did. I'll be free again a year from this Christmas. But then it's every man to his own taste. They'd never get me in the army while we still have a navy.....................

It's after 3:00 AM now. I'll be relieved of the watch in a few minutes and catch a couple hrs. sleep before reveille.

The next time you write send the letters to U. S. S. Preston #379, San Diego, California. It will reach me regardless of where I may be stationed.

Hoping to hear from you soon.

Sincerely, your brother Bill

***

In mid September, the Preston was ordered to the 180' dateline to escort the British battleship, Warspite to Pearl Harbor for minor repairs before she went on to Bremerton, Wash for extensive repairs. The Warspite had been damaged earlier in a Mediterranean battle. This was the first time the Preston was operating outside the company of other ships. Arrangements were made for the Preston and Warspite to exchange identification signals by radio when they came into first sightings. Since radio silence was in effect, this kind of communication between the two ships was remarkable. Return and arrival at Pearl Harbor was uneventful and repairs were soon begun to the battleship. Long closed sealed compartments were opened and the removal of bodies from the battle action, was undertaken. The Preston crew came aboard the Warspite to assist as needed. Friendships were formed between both crews before the Warspite left for Brernerton.

On October 4, 1941, the U.S. S. Preston sailed into San Francisco, then on to Mare Island to dry dock for repairs. According to orders, she would remain there until December 10. Bill was elated to be granted leave, and as soon as he was dismissed, he headed home to Minnesota by train. It would be so good to see his family once again and even better to be able to spend time with Annette.

What blessed relief it would be to stretch out once again in his bed upstairs and be able to sleep without interruption from the usual nighttime noises aboard ship. He had adapted to the lull of engine noise, but struggled at times in close quarters, with snoring shipmates.

The first Saturday that he was at home, Anna and her children came in mid-afternoon to share time with Karin, Bill, Jana and Lorraine. Anna stopped to pick up Katrina to include her in the visit.

Bill was pleased to see all of them and sat down on the floor to talk to the children. Anna brought oranges as a treat for everyone and she placed cut oranges on a plate next to the children where they were sitting. Little Anna and Eddie took their orange servings and began to eagerly eat the juicy fruit. Katrina was very quiet and just sat, looking around the room full of people that she didn't really know. Lorraine noticed Katrina just sitting, and said loudly, "I guess I'll just take her orange. She's not going to eat it anyhow."

Katrina did not want to eat an orange but at the same time she didn't want to lose it. She didn't know what to do and soon tears began to roll down her cheeks. Quickly Bill took the little girl on his lap, comforting her with words saying that "it was all right if she didn't want the orange."

A few minutes later, Jana brought out a box of chalk from the cupboard and took the children outside to draw on the sidewalk. They played together in this way for a while until Anna called them in to get washed up for an early supper. Shortly after the plates of food were set before the children, Lars and John walked in the back door.

"Hello, hello family," John called out in a loud voice. Once again Katrina's tears began as this boisterous voice frightened her. Soon she was sobbing in fear. Once again Bill came to her rescue, picking her up to comfort her. She sat on his lap quietly, once the tears subsided, as the rest of the family finished their meal.

"John, could I use your car to take Katrina back to the Anderleys?" Bill asked. "I think she needs to get back to familiar territory." After goodbyes from everyone, Bill walked Katrina to the car and they headed down the hill to Anderley's house.

Bill pulled into the long driveway next to the house, opened the door, and helped Katrina to the ground. He held her hand as they walked to the back door. After knocking, the door was opened by Selma and Katrina called out "Momma." Selma took Katrina's hand and led her into the kitchen. Katrina stopped to retrieve her teddy bear from where he sat in the rocking chair and hugged the toy to her chest.

"I'm afraid her visit didn't go very well with our family," Bill started to explain. "It was pretty overwhelming for her with so many people that she doesn't really remember."

Selma appraised the situation and decided that maybe Katrina needed supper to make things better. She and George had a later than usual supper that evening and they had just finished eating when Bill and Katrina returned. Katrina climbed into the chair at her usual place. Selma placed some boiled potatoes and a slice of meat on a plate and proceeded to cut the meat into small bites. "Better have some catsup for your meat and here's some corn," George offered. Selma poured gravy on Katrina's serving of potatoes, and the little girl eagerly began to eat, happy to be in her home once again.

Bill could see that Katrina was content again, back with this couple who loved her as their own. He sat down opposite Katrina with a cup of coffee and watched his little sister enjoying her meal. When he had finished his coffee, he stood up to leave. He walked over to Katrina and asked , "Can I have a hug before I go?" Katrina reached her arms to him and hugged as tight as she could. Selma walked Bill to the door, patted him on the back and said good bye, wishing him well. She thought he was such a wonderful young man, so caring towards his young sister. Silently she whispered a prayer for his safety. He deserved only the best in her opinion.

It was about seven o'clock in the evening as Bill made his way back to the Persson household. He drove past the Farmers Elevator and pictured in his mind, grain wagons and trucks waiting in line to dump their loads of corn. Soon the fields would be stripped and the land would settle down in all its nakedness to wait for winter. Some of the trees were already leafless but touches of color remained on the hillside oaks. The sumac clung tenaciously to its red leaves, grudgingly giving way to the season.

Going through the downtown area, Bill could see familiar stores that he remembered. There was Nichol's Variety, and on the next corner, Bachman's grocery. It seemed so long ago when he went in and out of those stores as a boy. And now just a few years later, he looked out on the town as a man.

A short time later, he parked John's car behind Lars', and walked back into the Persson house. Anna and her children were just getting ready to leave for home. Bill bent down to his small niece and nephew and collected hugs from them before they went out the door.

"We'll be back again before you have to leave," Anna called as she lead her young ones to the car. "I'll look forward to that," Bill answered. "Maybe I'll get to see Mel next time," he continued.

Bill noticed that Jana and Lorraine were already sitting by the radio in the front room. Lorraine was furiously turning the dial to get tuned into a favorite Saturday night radio show, "The Green Hornet." Lars was laughing at the effort, saying that he didn't stand a chance of hearing a boxing match when the "Hornet flew in."

Karin sat in her rocking chair, watching the girls settle into the radio show. John remained at the kitchen table having yet one more cup of coffee. Bill sat down with his brother and plans for their evening unfolded. Bill had called Annette the day before and they were going to meet as soon as her shift at Hank's was over. John suggested they take in a dance with him and a new girl he was dating, Marilyn Freeberg. Marilyn and Annette were cousins, and the arrangement of the four of them going out together would be a good time.

Bill went upstairs to change his shirt from what he had worn all day, splashed on some aftershave to complete his preparation for the evening. Soon he and John were out the door on the way to pick up Marilyn, who lived just outside of St. Peter. The next stop was at Hank's to pick up Annette. She was just opening her car door when John came to a stop next to her. Bill hurried out of John's car, ran over and swooped Annette into his arms. She was beautiful as she had been in his mind all these months, and a long saved kiss was firmly planted on her surprised mouth. "Hey there, sailor man," Annette said as she caught her breath, "I think you've missed me."

"Honey, you don't know the half of it," Bill responded. They climbed into the back seat and John continued the drive to Hardegger's, a dance hall by Lake Jefferson. Annette initiated conversation by asking, "How are you, Bill?" He answered with a kiss. "How long will you be home," she continued. He replied the same way with another kiss. At this point conversation was pointless she decided, so they just continued holding each other, savoring the closeness that they had both missed so much without realizing it before now.

As John wheeled to a stop in the dance hall parking lot, he called over his shoulder into the back seat, "Are you kids going to come in and dance a while or what?" Marilyn opened the front door on her side of the car, stepped out onto the gravel drive and said to Annette, "Meet me by the restroom door."

"I suppose we should go in. We are here to dance you know," Annette said to Bill. "Yeah, you're right. But it sure is fun just being in the car with you," he answered. Grudgingly they left the car and proceeded inside the dance hall.

Later when Bill thought back on this night, he couldn't even remember who was at the dance that evening. He and Annette shared every dance with each other, politely declining any offers to dance with someone else. When they did sit out a dance set, their conversation went on without pause, oblivious to anyone else in the dance hall. Bill did remember that the foursome stopped for breakfast at a small café in St. Peter before going to pick up Annette's car which remained parked at Hank's. As Bill and Annette got into her car, she jokingly said to John, "I'll see that he gets home before sunrise."

Every remaining night of his leave was spent with Annette. Bill hated to think that soon he would have to say goodbye to her and it would be a long, long time until they were together again. He did enjoy the days of being with his family, particularly seeing how his mother was recovering day by day, but his heart was with Annette now and she had become the person in his life that mattered the most. They decided to become engaged and before he left, he purchased a ring to make it official. Then much too soon it was time to leave and get back to navy routine aboard the Preston.

***

U. S. S. Preston #379

Oct. 19, 1941

Dear Mother,

Pretty slow about writing aren't I? Got back to the ship just a week ago today. Had a very nice trip back to Calif. Changed trains only once, at Omaha, Nebraska.

Met a lot of interesting people on the train. And of course a person gets acquainted quickly on a train anyway. So the 3 nights and two days I spent returning didn't see very long.

Stopped at Reno, Nevada for a few minutes Sat. nite but didn't get much chance to look around.

Got into Oakland, Cal. Sun. morning. Took a ferryboat over to San Francisco across the bay.

Didn't get much sleep on the train so I got a hotel room at 'Frisco and rested up a bit. Took a bath, etc. Went to a movie in the afternoon and then took a bus back to Vallejo & Mare Island and hunted up the good ship Preston.

It was rather nice to get back to work again after loafing around for a couple weeks. I'm certainly glad I was able to get those 12 days leave though. It was nice to get back home once more and see everyone.

I have the duty this Sat & Sun so I'm staying aboard ship and standing my watches. Feeling fine again now that I've had a chance to catch up on my sleep once more.

Couple of my shipmates & I made two liberties at 'Frisco this past week. We went over Tues. evening and also on Thursday evening. I like these big cities better because there's always so much doing there.

Guess I'll go ashore to Vallejo tomorrow night and go roller skating or something.

I've had several letters from Annette already since I got back. We write to each other nearly every day. You know how it is. Hope you're feeling better and can be up and around. Annette told me the night she met you that she thought you were grand. She and I agree on that. Hope you like her too. I don't think you could wish for a better daughter-in-law but maybe I'm prejudiced. Love does funny things to a guy.

I'll have to buckle down and really make a go of things. Now that I have so much more to work for than ever before.

The weather is almost as cool as it was back home today. It never does get very warm around here. So close to the sea and all that.

It's time for dinner now and I'll be off watch in a few minutes. I'm writing this while in the fireroom.

Give my best regards to all the family. Will write again soon.

Your loving son, Bill

***

USS Preston #379
Mare Island Calif.
Nov. 5, 1941
Dear Jana,

Have been looking for a letter from you, but haven't heard from you since I got back. Wrote to Mom once. Guess she got the letter…………………

I hear from my little blonde about three times a week. I mean Annette of course. So I get all the dope on what's going on. Seems like an awfully long time before I'll be coming back again. Longer now than ever. Still it will only be another year or a little more. Unless we get into the war.

Made a couple liberties over in Vallejo since I came back. That's the closest city from here. About a five minute ride on the ferry. Not much doing there tho, so I usually go over to San Francisco or Oakland when I go ashore. They are both large cities and always something doing there. A fellow can have a good time there. It's only about 35 miles from here. Ride the greyhound bus over. Only cost $1.25 round trip. Went over there last Saturday and stayed till Sunday night. It rained almost all the time but not very hard so I got by all right. Went to the movie "Sergeant York" last Sun. PM- and went roller skating in the evening.

Sure was fun to get roller skates on again. I used to do a lot of it when I was still at home before I joined the Navy if you remember.......................

Don't suppose you ever see Annette around, do you?

Have to go on watch now at 8:00 PM- won't get to bed till almost 1:00AM. So long for this time.

Your loving brother, Bill

***

U.S.S. Preston #379
Mare Island, Calif.
Nov. 20ᵗʰ, 1941
Dear Mother,

Will write a few lines so you'll know that I still exist. Hope you got the other letter I wrote since I came back.......... haven't heard from anybody back home for a month and a half. Beginning to feel like the unknown sailor. Annette is the only one who writes. I hear from her two or three times a week. She sure is a grand girl and I hope you liked her the evening I introduced her to you. It's hard to be separated though for such a long time.

I forgot completely about your birthday until I noticed the date when I started writing this letter. Anyway it's not too late to say, "Best birthday wishes". And may you have many, many more birthdays.

Suppose by this time it's getting pretty cold back in Le Sueur. It's chilly out here in the Bay area too. Had a light frost the other morning. It never does get very warm around San Francisco even in the summer.

I make most of my liberties in San Francisco. I was over there the last weekend over Sat & Sun. until Monday morning. Went to church over there last Sun. morning.

Know quite a few people over there now and always have a good time when I go there. Went over there last night again and got back to the ship at 7:30 this morning. Went up to see a girl that I met on the train (I also know her husband) on Saturday and talked and listened to the radio for a while and then she made some lunch. They took me for a ride around town afterwards and showed me a lot of interesting places around the city.

Also saw some other people I know after that. One lady invited me up to her house for Thanksgiving dinner today but I had the duty and had to get back to the ship this morning. We observed Thanksgiving today and had a very nice dinner aboard ship. We realize that there are a great many things for all the people in America to be thankful for.

.... Sure would like to hear from some of the family and find out how things are. Annette told me she saw Karl once at Hardeggers not so long ago. Annette's grandmother died a couple weeks ago and she felt pretty bad about it.

I'm feeling fine as ever and hope this finds all you folks the same.

Got a letter from the minister of the Lutheran church at St. Peter last week. He asked me to write how I'm getting along. I appreciate his interest.

Don't think we will be here at Mare Island very much longer but I'll write and let you know where they send us when we leave.

Didn't get any sleep last night so I'll have to go to bed for a couple hours. I've got the mid-watch tonight. From midnight till 4:00 A.M

Give my love to all and please ask Anna or Jana to write to me soon.

Your loving son, Bill

***

Shortly after Thanksgiving, Bill wrote to Karl, telling his brother about his engagement to Annette. He explained how during his last leave, they found out how much they really cared about each other. Annette was so different than all the other girls that he had known before. The girls he would take out while in port meant nothing to him. None of them had the special qualities that Annette had. He was sure that he wanted to spend the rest of his life with her and she told him that she felt the same way. Both of them were ready to focus on each other and start making plans for their future together. So they decided to take the next serious step and become engaged.

***

U. S. S. Preston #379
Mare Island, Calif.
Nov. 24, 1941
Hi Fella!

Grab a hold of something and don't let the shock throw you. My letters to you come about as often as Christmas. Don't know if this will reach you or not by the address I'm using but it should eventually. Say, it was tough that I didn't get to see you again when I was home on leave. But you know how it was. Such a short time at home and so many things to do and people to see. I tried to find you the day I went over to St. Peter and bought the ring for Annette, but you weren't at the shop and I didn't know where to look for you.

Annette keeps me pretty darn busy answering her letters in the spare time I do have. Being engaged is almost like being married. Did it surprise you when you found it out? Well I've grown up too, you know I'm not exactly running around in knee-pants anymore. When I get my hitch done in the navy I'll be all ready to settle down and be a domesticated stiff.. drop a line and let me know how things are stacking up for you. Still working for Otis? What's John doing? Don't know if he's still a civvy or out soldiering with the rest of the boys. Please write and let me know will you? ...... I think of you guys back there a lot ......

Had a letter from Anna today. First letter I've had from any of the family since I got back out here over a month ago. Don't know how much longer we will be here in the States but I guess it will be until after Christmas anyway. .....The weather out here is top except for a lot of fog and some pretty chilly mornings. It gets down to the freezing point some nights…………………..

When I bought the diamond at Johnson's Jewelry store in St. Peter, Ed Swanson was in there getting a watch fixed. He razzed the devil out of me about getting married. I'm getting used to being called a sucker about it but I still like the idea of spending the rest of my life with that little ash-blonde back in Le Sueur.

Hook, line & sinker. That's me! Don't forget that I want to hear from you. Soon please!

Your pal & brother, Bill

CHAPTER 10:

PEARL HARBOR

In the years of 1940-41, the "Great Debate" continued between the isolationists, who wanted to avoid entering another war, and the interventionists who deemed it best to send all possible aid the United States could afford, to enemies of Hitler and let them defeat Germany. The Japanese continued their advances in the Pacific to secure sources of oil, after President Roosevelt banned all exports of scrap iron, steel and oil to Japan to avenge their invasion of China. Diplomatic relations continued between the United States and Japan without either side doing much more than going through formalities.

In January of 1941 the US ambassador to Japan reported that Japan was planning to attack Pearl Harbor, the site of a large US Naval base. Unfortunately nobody in Washington took his report seriously. They refused to believe that Japan would dare attack the United States.

Japan was aware that if the United States entered a declared war against them, the US would be victorious since America had the largest naval force in the world at the time. But if Japan would strike first, they could destroy a large portion of the US Navy, and thus demoralize the United States, leaving them without power or will to retaliate. Japan firmly believed they could defeat the United States and so they developed a master plan to strike Pearl Harbor first.

Early on the morning of December 7, 1941 a Japanese mini-sub was spotted and sunk in Pearl Harbor. This event went unreported and a little more than an hour later over three hundred planes launched from six Japanese aircraft carriers began an attack that lasted two hours. The United States was caught by surprise, suffering the loss of close to three thousand military personnel and citizens. Five of eight battleships at Pearl Harbor were sunk or sinking. Two hundred airplanes that had been parked wing to wing on land were destroyed. The devastation was unbelievable.

The following day President Roosevelt asked Congress to declare war against Japan. His speech to the American public was forever memorable…….. "December 7, 1941, a date that will live in infamy."

****

U. S. S. Preston #379
Dec. 9th, 1941
Dear Mother,
Thought I'd better drop a line so you'll know that I'm still here and O.K in all respects.

I know it won't help to tell you not to worry about me because I know that you have been worrying a lot since the war started. But just the same it doesn't help matters any. It's hard for everybody. Just keep your chin up and everything will turn out all right just as it did after the last war.

Everything is censored before leaving and I'm not allowed to tell of our ship's movements. However I'll try to keep you informed as nearly as possible where I'm at and what I'm doing. Won't be able to write to you very often but that's to be expected under the circumstances.

Had one letter…. and that's all I've heard from home since I left last October. Can't understand why Jana doesn't write to me. She always used to before. It makes me feel as if everybody had forgotten me back home.

All except Annette. She's faithful to me. Writes a couple times a week.

Made a couple of liberties over in San Francisco since I last wrote. But haven't been over there since a week ago tonight. The last time I was ashore went to an opera that evening for the first time in my life. I enjoyed it very much.

Must be getting very cold back home now that winter has started. It gets cold here in California at night too but of course it's mild compared to the rigid climate of Minnesota.

Wrote to Karl some time ago but as yet haven't received an answer. Certainly would like to know where he and John are at and what they're doing. Suppose now that we are at war they will have to join or be called by either the Army or Navy.

Hope you aren't taking things too hard.

I'm pretty tired this evening, haven't gotten very much sleep the past three nights. Everything being naturally a little confusing.

I'll try to write a longer letter next time when things have cleared up some and we know more of what we will be allowed to write and what we won't.

If anyone at home should decide to write to me, my address will be only: Bill, U.S.S. Preston #379. C/o Fleet post office. Any mail should reach me by that address.

So long, Mother dear, for this time.

Your loving son, Bill

***

Repairs to the U. S. S. Preston at Mare Island were completed and the destroyer went underway for trials on December 10, 1941. News of the horrific December 7th attack on Pearl Harbor filtered down through the entire Navy force. Shock and disbelief were initial reactions from the officers to the enlisted men. Bill and his shipmates waited anxiously, hopeful of being called to some kind of avenging action. Instead they remained anchored in San Francisco until orders came for them to leave on December 16. They would be escorting a convoy to Pearl Harbor.

As they neared the mangled wreckage of Pearl Harbor, all those sailors who could find a place on the rail to watch the passage, did so. The devastation was beyond anything they could have imagined. Everyone stood silently as the Preston glided through the waters. The familiarity of this place they had been in and out of so many times was totally gone. This watery burial spot for so many comrades prompted them to stand at attention and salute and all did so without biding.

After finding docking space where they could refuel, the process began. On December 26 they departed once again for San Francisco. Hardly anyone even thought about the fact that Christmas had come and gone while they were at the site of such destruction.

The Preston navigated back and forth between San Francisco and San Diego during early January 1942. Then on January 10, they were assigned convoy escort duty to Pearl Harbor again. Their next duty was to escort two cargo ships, laden with war supplies and Army artillery troops to Christmas and Palmyra Islands, located about one thousand miles south of Hawaii. Bill thought it rather ironic that they were on Christmas Island on January 25 enjoying recreational time on the sandy beaches when just last month on the actual date of Christmas, they were gazing wide-eyed, on the destruction of Pearl Harbor.

***

U.S.S. Preston #379

January 31, 1942

My dear Mother,

Hope you haven't been doing too much worrying about me since I last wrote. As you see I'm very much alive and enjoying the best of health......

Got the Christmas card you sent more than a month after you sent it. Thanks.

Anna wrote to me at Christmas and sent a box of cookies and things. Got several letters and cards from people I don't even know after that notice in Dec. 10 issue of Le Sueur Herald, giving the names and addresses of us fellows in the Army and Navy. Even heard from Vivian.............

It's very XXX out here now. But I guess I'd rather have that the XXX XXX back home. It's pretty hard to write when the ship is rolling and pitching so much.

As you see by the papers, we are holding up and hope you folks back home are taking things as well. Nevertheless it will be a happy day when the war is over and we can return to peaceful pursuits again.........

...Get a copy of the Herald at times, though usually it's more than a month old when I get it. Still it's news to me and I think it's pretty nice of them to send it.

Hope this finds you in better health. Must close now as it's time for me to go on watch.

It may take a couple weeks before you get this because mail service is necessarily slow under present conditions.

Keep your fingers crossed and your chin up. I'll be coming home again sometime.

Your loving son, Bill

***

After returning to San Francisco on February 20, 1942, the next assignment for the Preston was escort duty involving the battleships <u>Pennsylvania</u> and <u>New Mexico</u> as they had gunnery practice off the California coast. Then the Preston headed for Puget Sound Navy Yard at Bremerton, Washington until February 26th, when they returned to San Francisco, this time providing escort for the <u>Maryland</u>. As this convoy moved through the waters heading south, Bill took advantage of off duty time and went to the mess room with a cup of coffee, sat down and wrote a letter to his little sister Lorraine.

***

U. S. S. Preston #379
Feb. 26, 1942
Dear Sister Lorraine,

This is the first chance I've had to answer your letter of January 6th. Was certainly glad to hear from you. Just received it a few days ago.

I'm in good health as ever. Haven't been sick a single day since I was home on leave last time. The Japs haven't been able to damage me yet either.

Finally got ashore once more the other day after having been aboard ship for almost two months. Believe me it sure felt good to get my feet back on solid ground again.

Got several letters from Annette the other day while in port. She told me that Karl had been drafted into the Army some time ago and that she thought he was now in Wyoming. That's the first I've heard about it. Can't even keep track of the family anymore. Karl hasn't written to me so I don't know his address. If you know what it is, would you please send it to me so I can write to him.

We run into lots of different kinds of weather these days in the navy, or maybe I should say climate. I've gotten to see quite a lot of this old world since the war started but of course I can't say where I've been or when either. Because that sort of information is censored.

Guess the people back home are beginning to feel the war now pretty much too. Now that there is shortages of a lot of things. For my part I can't squawk. Haven't had it much harder since the war started than I had it before. Or maybe it's just that I'm used to it after three years at sea duty. Anna wrote to me the other day. Said Jana was working at Rethwills again. She hasn't written since I was home in Oct. Guess I'll drop her a line soon and see if she answers.

There's not much more that I can say. Just "lots o' luck to you and everybody back home." I'll be coming home one of these days, I hope, when the shooting is over.

Love to all the family,
Your Brother Bill

***

The Preston remained in San Francisco from March 3, 1942 until April 15, getting underway five times to screen battleships during exercises. At times the repetitious drill got monotonous, yet if and when they headed to a battle situation, it was essential that all the ships knew how to function in war conditions. While Bill was on duty in the fire-room, it seemed at times all they did was circle round and round, back and forth. It was only during those times when he was able to be on deck that he could see and understand the movements of each ship as they practiced their maneuvers, learning their respective positions. Whenever he found himself approaching boredom, all he had to do was think about his past days of slogging through forests to build roads, or a frigid Minnesota morning in the barn milking cows. Navy life was good!!!

Since the onset of the war, people across the United States tried to demonstrate their appreciation to servicemen and women who were giving up so much while serving their country. While remaining on the home-front, citizens often wrote letters or sent cards to someone they didn't even know. In some cases, hometown newspapers sent weekly additions to anyone from their town. Bill was a grateful recipient of his hometown paper.

***

U. S. S. Preston #379
March 18, 1942
Dear Mr. Eastwood,
I have been receiving the Herald for several months now and am writing this to thank you for your kind consideration of us fellows in the service. Each copy of the paper is as welcome as a letter from home. Sometimes when my ship has been at sea a long time I get back copies that are a month or six weeks old, but most of the material is still news to me.

I've been in the navy for quite some time now. "Shipped in," December 1938, so you see I'm one of the "regulars."

See by your paper that the people back home are doing as much to win this war as we out here in the first line of defense, by conserving vital war materials, and in a lot of other ways too. It's good to know that the whole U.S. is behind us and that we're not fighting a lone battle that no one appreciates.

Have seen quite a lot of this old globe since I joined the fleet. Before the war I traveled from the East Coast through the "ditch" at Panama, from there across the equator to South America. Spent about a week in Ecuador. Of course all us "Pollywogs" were initiated and converted to "Shellbacks" when we crossed the line.

Done a lot of duty on the West Coast and Hawaii. Since the war, the movements of naval ships have been as secretive as the weather. So no comments on where we've been since then. I can say this though that most of us fellows in the navy don't need posters to help us remember Pearl Harbor. We'll jolly well remember it for a long time.

I'm not trying to do any recruiting work but if any of the boys back there are thinking of joining the Navy and want to know what it's like I can say for my part anyway that it's 4.0 (That's Navy slan- guage for 100% O.K!) Maybe I'm prejudiced, never having served in the Army or with the leathernecks, but I'm still cheering for the old Navy Blue.

The ship I'm on is a destroyer more commonly known as a tin-can among Navy men for obvious reasons that are self-explanatory. She rides as smooth as a Model T Ford, on a rubbing-board road, in rough weather, but the boat land-blubbers soon get used to that. It's the first twenty years that are the hardest. A "Boot" incidentally is to the Navy, what a "Rookie" is to the Army. You also soon get used to the idea that a torpedo may come nosing through the side some dark night and mess us up a bit, so we keep a sharp look-out, our fingers crossed and our powder dry.

We don't get much chance for recreation these days. Work before pleas- ure, you know, but when we do hit the beach we make up for lost time as anybody would do.

Here's hello, to the people of Le Sueur. If anyone cares to write me I'll try to give an interesting answer, though most everything is censored now-days.

Good luck and lots of success to the Herald and its staff. Thanks again for the free subscription.

Sincerely yours,

Bill Persson Fireman 1ˢᵗ Class, U. S. N.

***

U. S. S. Preston #379

Easter Sunday

April 5, 1942

Dear Mother,

Don't be too surprised but I finally did get around to writing home again. Must be about two months ago since I last wrote......

Annette writes to me once a week and of course I answer her letters, when I'm in port. That way I keep up on what's doing back there.

Get the Le Sueur Herald but then that's usually a month or two old by the time it reaches me.

I'm getting along just dandy. Best duty I've had since I joined the navy. Nothing of any importance has happened to me since I wrote last but even if it had, I wouldn't be allowed to write about it anyway so will just have to skip it. At any rate you know that I'm still in action and good health, which is the main thing I guess.

Have had two letters from Karl since he got in the Army. I wrote to him twice also. He knows what military life is like now and probably doesn't get such a big laugh out of it as he did when I used to come home on leave from the navy. Don't know if he's in Texas yet or not, haven't heard from him for awhile. Hope he's O.K. and wish him lots of luck. We'll probably all need a lot of it before the shooting is over.

Have the duty today so had to stay aboard. Was ashore yesterday though. Have been going ashore a great deal the last month or so. Have quite a few friends in the city now, and always manage to have a pleasant time when I go over. Yesterday I went to a birthday party at a place about 17 miles from here. We had a steak dinner in the evening and had a good time.

We have been having a lot of rain lately out here. It's showering again today. Liquid sunshine.

Suppose everything is green and growing back in Minnesota by now. We usually have such nice weather the year 'round in the places I'm at in the navy that I don't appreciate spring like I used to when I was back home.

Had another birthday last month as you well know. Don't feel any older though. Twenty-three years young. Getting right up there, huh?

Got a cigarette lighter from the American Legion Post in Le Sueur last week. I think they sent one to each of the boys in the service. I sent a card and thanked them for it.

Annette sent me a very nice framed picture of herself for my birthday. I bought a Gruen wristwatch for her three days ago and sent to her for graduation. She doesn't graduate from teachers training yet for about 6 more weeks or so but I wanted to get it early so she would be sure to get it in time. It was a $37.50 watch so guess it should be O.K.

We're getting a little higher pay now since the war. I make $82.00 a month. But everything is so much higher that it doesn't go any farther than it did when I was making less. I'll have to pay between 30 & 50 dollars in income tax for this year unless they change it to a higher percentage.

They started giving us service men free postage yesterday so I won't have to bother with stamps now when I write .....

Have been having good chow even during the war. Eat better than a lot of the civilians do I guess, in port anyway. Of course when we're at sea for a long time we don't get as much fresh food as in port but it's still pretty good. Can't kick on it. Today we had ham for breakfast and fresh milk. For dinner we had veal, ice cream and pie.

I understand that the families back home who have members in the service get service flags. Have you got one each for Karl and I? What do they look like? Karl mentioned something about it in his last letter that you had two flags in the window, one for the army and one for the navy.... Have heard from Anna several times since I was home last Oct. Expect I'll hear from her again soon. Have an occasional letter from Annette's sister, Irene. She is working .... In Ohio. Had two letters from Harriet Larson of Winthrop, Minn. Don't know her but she wrote to me and I answered. Guess she went to high school at Le Sueur

Have some more letters to write this afternoon so will sign off for this time. Hope you are all in good health at home. Well, try to write sooner next time.

Your loving son, Bill

P.S. Address:
U.S.S.Preston #379
C/o Postmaster
San Francisco, Calif

***

U. S. S. Preston #379
April 8, 1942
Dear Jana,
Received your letter a couple days ago, so I'd better make an attempt to answer it.

Seems like when a person writes often there's a lot to write about but when you let it go for a long time there just isn't anything.

Finally wrote to Mom a couple days ago. Just have a bad habit of putting things off until tomorrow.

Had two letters from Karl since he got in the Army, but haven't heard from him for some time now. He's probably been transferred to some other place. He sent me a couple snapshots of himself in uniform.

Have had good duty for the past month or so. Almost get more liberty than I can use. Not more than I can use, but more than my pay day can stand. Went ashore on my birthday too and had a good time.

I'm writing this at sea so you maybe won't get it for some time. Won't be mailed until we get into port you know.

Sent a letter to the Le Sueur Herald sometime ago. I guess they published it, because I got a letter from Annette just before we went to sea and she sure gave me the razzberries about it. .....

On one side of the paper she wrote the kind of letter that she usually does, and then introduced me to Miss Annette Griep as a local Le Sueur girl who would like very much to correspond with the sailor whose letter she saw in the Herald. While on the other side she wrote a typical pen-pal letter. Will have to answer it though and tell her what the score is. All in fun of course, because we get along like two bugs in a rug. Couldn't hardly quarrel being a couple thousand miles apart.

I sent her a wrist watch last week for her graduation this spring so she should have it by now. Also wired her some flowers for Easter. Don't know if she got them or not. Said she had ten days vacation. I suppose you had an Easter vacation too.

Well next month is Mother's Day. Have you any idea what Mom would especially want? If you know I wish you would write and tell me right away so I would have time to pick it out and send it. Please do. Also what do you think Lorraine would like for her birthday? You'd be doing me a big favor if you'd tell me, because I never know just what to buy for anybody.

I'm getting nowhere fast with this letter. Can think of a lot of things to write but then we have to be careful of what we say these days. At least you know now that's I'm still in circulation and feeling fit and mean as ever. Right now I'm itching to get ashore again. Nothing like a little shoreside to get a sailor back in good humor. Every liberty in the navy is like Saturday night on the farm. All hands whoop it up and no holds barred.

Bet it's nice back in Minnesota now that spring is here. Wish I could be home for a few days. We have nice weather almost all the time here so don't appreciate spring like you do back there. When you write use this address, U.S. S. Preston #379 c/o Postmaster San Francisco, Calif.

Hope this finds you well. My regards to the family.

Your brother, Bill

***

On May 19, 1942, the U. S. S. Preston left Puget Sound, refueling in Seattle. Her duty this time was to escort the aircraft carrier, <u>Saratoga</u> during operations in the Strait of Juan de Fuca. This Strait is about 102 miles long and ten to eighteen miles wide, lying just south of Vancouver Island.

Bill wrote to his mother several days after they had traversed Juan de Fuca Strait. He sat topside whenever he was off-duty and wrote home later, wishing that he might mention his "cruise" as the convoy maneuvered these waters. Later when they had met Task Force Sixteen, the transferring of planes and bombs was interesting to observe too. Of course any information about transferring war materiel was censored so the comments in his letters were strictly chatter about his life, avoiding any mention of wartime activity that might provide naval intelligence to the enemy.

…One doesn't realize how grand it is to get back on land again after having been at sea nearly a month….. Always go to see one friend or the other while ashore. Doesn't make any difference to them if I have quite a bit of money or if I'm broke……. Guess that's the true test of a friend……Got three letters from Annette the other day when my ship came into port after a long time at sea…….The place where we are now

has very nice weather. It's neither too hot nor too cold. Just invigorating. Cool enough so I can use a jacket on the top-side and cover with a blanket at night. Too bad I can't tell you where I am or where I have been. Not that it matters very much I don't suppose…. Haven't been seriously ill since 1939 when I had appendicitis. As long as the Japs don't give me lead-poisoning, I'll be all right……..   *Your loving son, Bill*

***

U. S. S. Preston 379
June 23rd, 1942
Dear Mother,

Haven't written to you since May 20th so will attempt a line or two. Wrote to Anna the other day so if you read that letter there really isn't much to say.

At least you'll know now that I'm still around and feeling fit as a fiddle. Those slant eyed Japs haven't knocked me off yet. Not by a jugful.

Had a letter from Karl a while back. Said that he expected to get a few days furlough sometime this month. Hope he has been able to and come home for at least a little while I mean. Would be nice if one of your sons could get home even though I won't be able to until after the war…..

I've been ashore on liberty a couple times since we got to this port but didn't have very much fun. So many people here that you can't hardly move in the city and then our liberty expires at sunset so it doesn't hardly pay to go over to town for such a short time and have so much trouble trying to get transportation and everything.

Suppose by now the pea-pack at the factory has started. Would like to be back there in a way but on the other hand, there's easier ways than that to make a living. Maybe the navy has made me soft but I just can't ever imagine myself going back to work on a farm or for the M.V.C.Co.

Perhaps I'll come back there to live someday. I'm sure I don't know now. Guess Annette would have a little say-so about where we're going to live and she seems to think that Minnesota is the only place. For my part I like the West Coast. Everything seems to be more lively out there than back in the middle west.

I should write to both Lorraine and Jana…. After I've written to you and Ann there doesn't seem to be much to say without repeating myself……………….

Can't think of anything else right now so best of everything to you Mother dear. Hope your health has improved.

Your loving son, Bill

***

By the summer of 1942, the Japanese plan to take Port Moresby in New Guinea, then set up airfields in the southern Solomons became apparent. This position would hamper and hopefully deter, the United States naval attempt to move planes, guns and troops in the Pacific, particularly from Australia where the U. S. had already set up supply bases as they prepared a counter attack to the devastating Pearl Harbor assailment.

Construction began hurriedly to build an airfield on Guadalcanal, a strategic position to the Japanese defensive plan against any such counter attack by the United States.

While the south Pacific was abuzz with war plans and build-up by the Japanese and the US, the Preston continued with escort duty back and forth between Pearl Harbor, San Francisco, San Diego, Seattle and back to Pearl Harbor again. After all they had practiced during maneuvers, the entire crew was more than ready for action. But their duty remained at providing escort service. At times it seemed that being an escort wasn't that important to the war effort, but it truly was in view of the major losses that had been suffered on December 7. It was essential that the naval ships afloat be protected against possible attack, especially since repairing damaged ships and building new ships took time to complete, and time was of the essence. Still Bill and so many of his shipmates wondered if they would ever get a chance to use their warfare skills.

***

U. S. S. Preston #379

Sept. 21ˢᵗ, 1942

Dear Mother,

It's been so long since I last wrote to you that I don't hardly know how to start out, and when I do get started there's so little that I'm allowed to write about.

Funny isn't it, how a person keeps putting off until tomorrow what could be so easily done today. Here I've been intending to write to you every time I have a little spare time and just never get around to it until now. I think of you every day, Mom, so even if you don't hear from me very often you still know that you're always in my heart.

Karl and I have been writing to each other since he got in the army. Suppose he told you that when he was on furlough. Was nice for him to be able to get back for a few days so that you at least got a chance to see one of us boys. Wish I could have been home at the same time, but guess I won't be able to come home till after the war is over. Will be a year next month since I was in Le Sueur last. Quite a while at that. .... I've been just too busy to be thinking of it too much. We keep on the go now you know.

Wrote to Anna this evening also. Trying to get caught up on my letter writing. I owed her a letter for several weeks.

Hear from Annette nearly every week. That is when my ship is in port and the mail comes in. She should be teaching school by now, over at Kasota. Sent her a Parker pen & pencil set for her birthday last month and a Gruen wristwatch for graduation last June. Wish we could be together, but then there's no use in wishing, just have to take it like everybody else does. Maybe it's all for the best at that. Annette told me that you had heard that the Preston was sunk and that you were worried about me. We're still very much afloat and going strong.

The weather here is disagreeably warm the year 'round and a guy does a lot of sweating standing the hot watches. It's 11:00 P.M. now. I worked until 9:00 o'clock this evening but don't have to stand a watch tonight so I'll get a lot of sleep for a change. I've gotten so used to being on watch at all hours of the day and night that I can sleep anyplace whenever I have time to do it……..

Bought a few small war bonds lately, that's about the only way I can hang onto any money. Bought a new uniform of tailor-made blues for $36.00. Haven't had a chance to wear them yet. Sold my old uniform. I had it for three and a half years and it was getting rather shabby.

Well, Mom, there's not much more that I can think of right now. I'm getting along fine and haven't been sick.

Say "Hello" to Dad and girls for me. Hope you are all well.

Your loving son, Bill

***

USS Preston #379
September 21, 1942
Dear Sis, (to Anna)
My conscience after all these weeks finally got the best of me. Just had to drop you a couple lines to let you know that I'm O.K.

Heard from Karl a while back, just after he got back to camp from his furlough. From what he says he must have had a pretty good time while he was back there. Wish I could get a couple weeks leave again. It's been almost a year now since I was back last. Right on your birthday for the last two years. Remember? Well, don't look for me this year.

I made another rate the first of this month. I'm Boilermaker second class now, which is one pay grade above Fireman 1/c. It's an extra $24.00 *a month which isn't such a bad raise. Karl made his corporal rate pretty fast. I suppose he's angling for sergeant now.*

Annette mentioned in one of her last letters that mother had heard rumors that the Preston was sunk. I don't know where all that stuff starts but it sure gets around fast. We are still very much afloat and intend to stay that way.

This war is pretty dull as far as I'm concerned, but I'm not growling. I'd much rather be alive than be a dead hero. Like one fellow put it "it's not dying for your country that counts, it's making the enemy die for his country first that counts."

Suppose it's getting pretty cool evenings back home now. Could certainly use some cool weather where I am right now. These watches here do get awfully hot at times, and it doesn't even cool off at night so I can sleep in comfort.

Don't remember when I wrote to you last but can't say where I've been anyway so it doesn't make much difference. Enough to say that I've been in some good liberty ports and some bum ones, some good duty and some bad. Like a civilian job it has its ups and downs.....................

Annette complains that Le Sueur isn't what it used to be. Must be that too many of the eligible escorts are being drafted. The last letter I had from her she said the town was full of Mexicans, Indians and "wolves." Don't know just who the "wolves" were.

Annette should be teaching school out at Kasota by now. Don't envy her that job either........

I don't know why it's so hard to think of something to say, but it is. Anyway, say hello all from me...

Your brother, Bill

***

A few weeks later Bill once again wrote to Anna. He mentioned that their first cousin, Everett Johnson was also in the Navy. Bill was pleased to have heard from Everett and even more pleased to learn that he was also a navy man! It seemed eons ago that the Persson and Johnson families gathered to share holidays or other family celebrations. Now the older cousins were all grown up and scattered across the world, seeing places they had only imagined as school children.

***

USS Preston

Oct. 5th, 1942

Dear Sis, (to Anna)

Got your letter yesterday so will make some attempt to answer it.

Already wrote two letters tonight and that's quite a bit for me considering what a chore I make of writing letters. Wrote to Annette of course and also to Everett Johnson.

I got a letter from Everett yesterday and darn near fainted when I found out that he was in the navy too. Well the boys don't have much choice these days, either join the navy or marines or the army gets 'em. If the army ever tried to get me when I was a civilian there'd be two guys missing, me and the guy they sent after me. They'd find me at the nearest navy recruiting station.

But then I've been over all that and it's through. Will have my first cruise finished soon and start on the second.

Wish I could have some of that cool weather you mention. It's so hot here that a person is always sweating. We're starting to get a little rain now although for the past week or so but it doesn't cool off very much. The only way you can tell when winter comes is that it rains more than in the summer.

A year ago now since I was home last. Wish I could be in Le Sueur again this fall for a while but that's out of course.

Guess I told you that I made Boilermaker 2/c last month, so don't find that there's much to write about. Things are going along smooth enough. Lots of watches and lots of work. Now and then a liberty for a few hours on the beach where a guy can get a beer or two if he's aggressive enough and a little bigger than the rest of the guys shoving in line.

I've been trying to get a snapshot or photo of myself to send to several people but it's just about impossible. The studios are jammed every day and when I get around to renting a camera they're all sold out in that size film. If I to manage to get one though, I'll send you one.

Guess that's about all for now. Write again, and do it more often. As always, Bill

***

While it was impossible to personally know all of the 248 enlisted men aboard the Preston, each work unit developed their own sense of camaraderie as they went about their duty. The "black gang" serving in the fire-room, was no exception. Since these men worked together in close quarters, it was easy to become better acquainted. They shared news from home with each other, enjoying the good times, commiserating over the not so good ones.

Bill considered John Lisak, Edward Newsome and Aaron Scott to be three of his best buddies. Johnny was married, and his wife Margaret lived in their San Diego apartment while John served on the Preston. Many times while in port at San Diego, Bill was invited to their home for meals. Ed was married also and he had recently shared a joyful letter from his wife Nancy, back in Pennsylvania, telling about the birth of their first child, a little boy. Aaron and Bill were the "bachelors" of this group, although following Bill's engagement to Annette, he was considered almost married. "The Kid" as Aaron was called, was just eighteen, so any thoughts of commitment that he might have had, remained in the distant future.

On August 31, 1942, these four sailors were together in port at Pearl Harbor. Coincidentally they happened to share a liberty together, and so they headed for the nearest bar to enjoy a few beers before it was time to return to their ship.

Ed spotted a table in the back of the bar and they threaded their way through the crowd of sailors to find chairs together. Once they were seated, Ed announced, "The first one's on me to celebrate the birth of my son." The others reciprocated in turn, and with each round of drinks, the conversation changed from loud, happy joking and laughing, to a more somber tone.

Johnny began his speculative thoughts by asking, "Do you think we'll finally get to see some action when we leave Pearl?" Ed answered by saying, "Scuttlebutt says we're heading for the Solomons." Bill went on to add, "I think we're more than ready for some real action." Aaron sat quietly for a moment, then asked, "Don't you guys ever get scared?" Three heads nodded in unison as this seriousness overtook the conversation. Bill broke the weighty silence by saying, "Well, Kid, all we can do is say our prayers, keep the engines running, and hope for the best!"

CHAPTER 11:

ON TO THE SOLOMONS

In 1568 a Spanish explorer discovered a group of islands, lying east of New Guinea. Further exploration of the land led to the discovery of gold. The explorer thought that this gold might have been used in building the Temple of King Solomon in Jerusalem and so named these islands, the Solomon Islands.

Nearly four hundred years later, a consideration more valuable than the earlier claims to gold, became apparent. It was location. As the Japanese advancing war efforts continued, all evidence showed how important it was for them to possess and control the Pacific Islands of this area. At all costs they wanted to insure that supply and communication routes were stemmed to prevent the Allies from operating out of bases in Australia and other key positions.

Guadalcanal Island, one of the southern Solomon Islands, is one of the largest in the British Solomon Island Protectorate. The land mass is over two thousand square miles, populated by numerous island peoples, primarily a dark-skinned tribal group known as Melanesians. The Japanese took control of Guadalcanal through an invasion in May of 1942. On August 7, 1942 the Allies began the attack to drive the Japanese out of this area. This offensive, caught the Japanese off- guard. Stunned and surprised; they later made several attempts to regain control of the partially constructed airfield there. (The US called this airfield, Henderson Field)

On October 16, 1942, the Preston sailed from Pearl Harbor, bound for the Solomons, as part of Task Force 16. After rendezvousing with

Task Force 17, both forces combined to become Task Force 61 which included; <u>USS Enterprise</u> (carri<u>er), USS South Dakota</u>(battleship), heavy cruiser <u>USS Portland,</u> anti-aircraft cruiser <u>San Juan,</u> and eight destroyers; Porter, Mahan, Cushing, Preston, Smith, Maury, Cunyngham and Shaw. Later TF 61 combined with TF 63, which then was called TF 61 collectively, and included eighty-two ships.

As the ships neared the Santa Cruz Islands, news of an attack on the force was reported. About an hour before daybreak, October 26, 1942, all hands on the Preston were ordered to battle-stations. Bill rolled from his bunk, bounded up topside, to take his place manning the hoses as a part of damage control. The adrenalin was pulsating through all the Preston sailors. After months and months of practice, at last they might be a part of the real war. Everyone was on edge and anxious for the fight to begin. By 11:00AM , the carrier <u>Hornet</u> reported being under attack by dive bombers and torpedo planes. Her returning planes were diverted to the <u>Enterprise</u>.

Soon the onslaught of enemy planes began. The Preston's orders were to provide screening to the <u>Enterprise</u> on her starboard side. A Japanese dive bomber made a run at the Preston, sending a bomb much too close to the starboard quarter. All the months of training exploded in a barrage from the Preston's guns. So much ammunition had been expended, that at one point the gunnery officer called a cease fire in order to clear the empty shell casings. It was later reported that 350 rounds of 5" caliber and 2460 rounds of 20 mm ammunition had been fired during the attack by this vessel.

In addition to the danger from the enemy plane guns, one ship had been torpedoed and the fear that more would be hit reverberated throughout the force.

After a brief lull in the action, the remaining Japanese planes once again focused their firing on the <u>Enterprise</u>. The Preston laid a barrage of 5" bursts above the carrier towards the planes but not before the <u>Enterprise</u> took a devastating hit amid-ship.

The third wave of the enemy attack took place about eleven fifteen. It was estimated that over one hundred seventy enemy planes took part in the attack on the Hornet and Enterprise.

After losing fifty six planes to anti-aircraft guns on US ships and planes launched from the carriers, the Japanese left the area. Most of the American pilots and crew members shot down into the ocean were saved, eight being rescued by the Preston. Bill was able to watch with interest as Lt. R. S. Merritt and two crew members from the Hornet were taken aboard. All the rescued personnel's injuries were quickly assessed and treated as best they could be under battle conditions.

At two o'clock, orders came down to set sail for Noumea, New Caldonia. Commander Max C. Stormes ordered the Preston to proceed at 29 knots in order to retake Task Force 16. Once out of the battle area, headed southward towards "peaceful waters" again, it was hard to imagine that just a few hours before, they had been in a heated exchange.

Just after getting underway to New Caldonia, Bill reported to the fire-room for his shift. For the first time since joining the "black gang", he wished his duty was topside. It had been so exciting to be on deck when the battle was going on. The loudness of the guns still echoed in his ears and he'd never forget the sight of enemy planes being shot from the skies. But it was back to a normal routine now and his duty called to him from below decks.

As Bill was about to step through the hatch into the fire-room, the chief boilermaker Ralph Gilmore approached him and said, "I could have used you in here today, sailor. I had to tell the men how to do their job. They were un-nerved by all the noise from the guns." Bill answered jokingly, "Aw, chief. We maneuvered around just fine without me. It depends on whose hand you want to hold, mine or some other gob!" The chief left the area with one final hrumph as he headed towards his quarters.

The shift hours passed quickly and soon this watch was over. Bill and the others on duty headed to their bunks to catch some sleep before beginning a new day. It was 6:15 AM when Bill awoke after a restless night of tossing and turning, all the while going over and over in his head the battle he experienced yesterday. He decided that he might as well get up since he couldn't sleep anyhow. He got dressed for the day, and headed to the mess-room for breakfast. He went through the early morning chow line, then looked around the room for a familiar face. He spotted a gunners mate that he had met once while on liberty in Frisco. Bill set his tray down on the table across from Ed Kirchberg and said, "Good job shooting today, sailor." Kirchberg looked up to see who was sitting down, shook his head from side to side and answered, "I can't hear a thing you're saying. The guns are still going in my head." Bill nodded in understanding and turned his attention to the plate of scrambled eggs before him.

Both men finished their food in silence about the same time, then with a parting wave to the other, headed out of the mess-room. Bill decided to go topside to see what he might see as they sailed towards the port of Noumea.

It soon became apparent that they were nearing land. The deep blue of the ocean lightened progressively to a beautiful turquoise color as the waters grew shallow. Low-slung hills came into sight, then in the distance Bill could just make out the white lighthouse standing sentinel onshore. As the ship drew closer and closer to this natural harbor, Bill realized that what he had called "hills" were in fact a band of low mountains that rose abruptly just beyond the city.

As they entered the channel, rows of tiled roofed houses attested to the fact that this port was a sizeable city with a busy commercial harbor, only recently changed by the presence of all kinds of Navy ships. A number of merchant freighters and at least thirty fishing boats shared harbor space with the allies.

Bill thought back to his younger days, working for Cy Gunders, and how he had enjoyed looking through Cy's old National Geographic magazines. And now here he was, soon to land on one of those South Pacific Islands he had wished to see someday. Wouldn't it be something to actually view one of those jungle natives? "Wait a minute," Bill said to himself, "what am I seeing here?"

He looked again to be sure his eyes weren't deceiving him, but yes, it was so. There on the dock, coming out of a warehouse door, was a Melanesian native. He was National Geographic perfect, complete with a bone in his nose, nearly red hair frizzled about his head, shell necklaces hanging down his chest and wearing, what appeared to be, an orange skirt.

The sight of this jungle man, ambling along the dock, against the backdrop of the tiled roofed homes of the of European settlers, made it hard to remember the reason the Preston had come to Noumea, New Caldonia. It was not a pleasure trip! There would be no visit to a primitive jungle village or learning how Europeans came to this area. The Navy was here to re-arm, then leave to face the unknown near another pacific island.

For several days, the Preston remained at anchor in the harbor, awaiting their turn to dock and take on necessary stores and ammunition. As they waited, the sailors were put to work; scraping this, painting that, polishing something , stowing whatever; keeping as busy as possible during their time in Noumea. Once docked, the loading operations began, a job shared by all available hands.

On November 8, 1942 the Task Force was once again underway, this time heading northwest towards Guadalcanal. From enlisted man to officer, all thoughts were on what lay ahead of them. When the next battle took place, would their luck hold? Would they be in that number who would regroup when the guns were silent again?

The focus on Guadalcanal was to enable the U. S. Navy to transport troops and supplies to their beleagured military, who were fighting continual jungle battles on the island against the Japanese stronghold. The Japanese also needed to bring in more soldiers to defend and enlarge their holdings on the island. As the Task Force drew closer to Guadalcanal, ships were assigned escort duty to various landing craft. On November 10th, the Preston was one of two destroyers detached to escort the minesweeper Southard, as she landed the 2nd Marines behind enemy lines.

The fierce Naval Battle of Guadalcanal began on November 13 during the very early morning hours, with opposing forces firing at each other at very close range. It was extremely difficult to distinguish between friend and foe. The confrontation took place southeast of Savo Island and lasted less than half an hour. (Savo Island lies just northeast of the northern tip of Guadacanal) The Japanese retreated before they could attack the strategic Henderson Field. Two US destroyers were lost during this melee.

After midnight on November 14, the Japanese convoy returned to strike again by bombarding Henderson Field on Guadalcanal. By dawn, the Marine and Naval aircraft from Henderson Field and also aircraft from the approaching Enterprise took action against the Japanese. Yet in spite of heavy losses, the Japanese reinforcements continued to steam towards the battle zone to begin their assigned task of landing troops and supplies. The US Forces remained strongly determined to prevent this.

The calendar in the mess-room noted the day as November 14, 1942. Bill reported for the evening watch at 11:45PM. An air of tension prevailed throughout the ship, topside and below. Everyone was thinking about the next encounter with the Japanese and what the outcome might be.

As Bill stepped through the air-locked hatch into the fire-room, he was met by Chief Gilmore. Soon Boilermakers Lisak, Newsome and Scott joined Bill as they relieved the men coming off the second "dog watch." Chief Gilmore announced that he was staying in the fire-room for a while with this relief crew. He had been informed earlier, that by midnight, the Preston would be one of several ships detached from TF 16, operating as TF 64. Their position would be in this order: destroyers USS Walke, USS Benham, USS Preston, USS Gwin, followed by battleships USS Washington and USS South Dakota.

The men began their watch by performing a system of checks to make certain the boilers were functioning perfectly and remained that way. This was absolutely essential in order to execute different speeds and directions as further orders came down.

Once the chief felt confident that the engines and crew were in perfect functioning modes, he left the fire-room, saying that he would return later that night to check on their progress. He would never be able to live up to those parting words.

When the air-locked hatch was closed again, the only sounds heard were that of the churning engines. Aaron Scott, "the Kid", broke the men's silenceby joking, "I thought he'd never leave!" Smiles came from all, then silence returned as each man focused on the job at hand. Soon they felt the movements of the ship as she swung into position and increased her speed to 23 knots as ordered.

"Well, guys. It feels like we're getting in line now," Bill said. Simultaneously each man offered a prayer in his own words. Now all they could do was hope for the best.

Just after midnight, the two battleships opened fire on a target off their starboard beam. The next to fire was the Walke, target again to starboard. Around 12:30 AM, the Preston found and fired on a target off their starboard bow. All her guns were directed towards an enemy ship that was seen by the look-outs on this clear, moon- lit night.

As soon as the guns began, the noise level below deck rose upward in incredible crescendo. As the men worked feverishly to maintain power and speed, it seemed to grow ever louder.

The Preston continued firing and her targeted enemy ship burst into flames. Those watching the fireworks gave out a collective cheer before their sight and attention was redirected to yet another Japanese ship. Once again a salvo was directed towards the enemy and within seconds, return fire rocked the Preston, hitting her with two six inch shells. One shell sped directly into the fire-room, on her starboard side. Suddenly all previous fire-room noise was ended and there remained nothing but deathly silence .... The amidship area was littered with debris from the hit that toppled the Number 2 stack, which landed over a torpedo tube. All frenzied action to aid the wounded and fight the fires that threatened the TNT of the torpedo heads, went unheard in what was once the fire-room......................

The second projectile to hit the Preston did not explode, but killed a crewman and tore a huge hole in the deck. While all of this action was happening at starboard, an enemy cruiser drew in on the crippled Preston on her port side. The salvo of eight inch shells left the deck a mangled, burning wreck. Amid the destruction, sailors were bombarded by flying cabbages, potatoes and canned goods as the ships stores were struck. A few minutes later, the order to abandon ship was given, and quickly, in less than ten minutes time, the Preston silhouetted in the moonlight, slipped silently to the bottom of Iron Bottom Sound.

One hundred thirteen enlisted men and four officers were lost with the Preston during this Naval Battle of Guadalcanal, including Nels Axel William.

***

The Commander of the South Pacific Force, Admiral William F. Halsey, later eulogized those lost at Guadacanal by saying:

"To the superb officers and men on land, on sea, in the air and under the sea who have performed such magnificent feats for our country in the last few days X You have written your names in golden letters on the pages of history and won the undying gratitude of your countrymen X My pride in you is beyond expression, no honor for you could be too great X

Magnificently done X God Bless each and every one of you X to the glorious dead: Hail Heroes! Rest with God X signed Halsey" 88

***

The little girl sat on Selma's lap in the large wooden rocking chair. Katrina was four, and much too big to sit and be rocked, but today Selma understood the child's need to be held close. The news had come telling of a Naval battle half way around the world. Bill's ship was lost early in the morning of November 15, 1942 and Bill had gone down with his ship. Selma needed to hold and comfort Katrina as much as she needed to feel comfort herself. Selma's heart ached for this little girl, sharing her loss. Now Katrina would have only a passing memory of her brother in his sailor suit, remembering for years how scratchy the Navy blue wool had felt against her face. She clutched her silver dollar, the "cartwheel" that Bill had given to her.

As they sat together, the squeaky rocking chair kept time to Selma's soothing song…

"Oh, where have you been, Billy Boy, Billy Boy? Oh where have you been charming Billy?"

CREDITS

Letters of: Nels Axel William Strand, Arvid Strand, Cliff Strand

U. S. S. Preston in WWII- E. Andrew Wilde, Jr. Commander, USNR Ret.
Documents, Recollections & Photographs

Wartime Deployment of the USS Preston DD-379
(Deck Log and War Diary entries)

Wikipedia- Savo Island, Guadalcanal Island, Task Force 61, Attack on Pearl Harbor

Buzzle.com- Japanese in WW II

The Bluejacket Manual- 14th Edition

The Old Breed- E.B. Sledge

Personal Interviews with Preston Survivors:
Edward William Kirchberg S1c
George Robert Nealis RM3c

Written notes from Preston Survivors:
Charles Parker Calhoun RM1c
James Howard Spillman Sc2c

Personal Recollections:
Ann Tellijohn, Jeanie Lopez, Cliff Strand,
Other Strand family members, The Author

Technical Advice:
Clayton Strand, Tony C., Joe K.

Editors: Family members, my friend Karen